Welcoming the or

Welcoming the Japanese Visitor

INSIGHTS, TIPS, TACTICS

KAZUO NISHIYAMA

A Kolowalu Book
University of Hawai'i Press
Honolulu

01 00 99 98 97 96   5 4 3 2 1

Library of Congress Cataloging-in-Publication Data
Nishiyama, Kazuo.
    Welcoming the Japanese visitor : insights, tips, tactics / Kazuo
Nishiyama.
        p.   cm.
    "A Kolowalu book."
    Includes bibliographical references and index.
    ISBN 0–8248–1759–1 (pbk. : alk. paper)
    1. Tourist trade. 2. Visitors, Foreign. 3. Travelers—Japan.
I. Title.
G155.A1N56   1996
338.4'791—dc20   95–46072
                                                       CIP

Chapter 9 illustrations by Yuko Green

University of Hawai'i Press books are printed on acid-free
paper and meet the guidelines for permanence and durability
of the Council on Library Resources

Book design by Paula Newcomb

Contents

Foreword

Welcoming the Japanese Visitor by Professor Kazuo Nishiyama provides the reader with practical and useful advice on how to effectively market tourism products and services to Japanese visitors. Professor Nishiyama's work is based on long and successful first-hand involvement and research on international tourism in Hawaii and beyond.

The School of Travel Industry Management at the University of Hawaii at Manoa welcomes Professor Nishiyama's newest publication because we believe that a good understanding of Japanese visitors by host nationals not only provides economic benefits but also promotes goodwill and mutual understanding between Japan and other countries. In 1993 Japan ranked as the world's third largest outbound country, after the United States and Germany. Nearly 18 million Japanese visitors traveled around the world, spending in excess of $30 billion, or approximately 10 percent of the world total. In Hawaii, Japan now represents the single largest segment of all international arrivals, accounting for 1.7 million visitors and $3 billion in expenditures, or nearly 25 percent of all arrivals and 30 percent of all revenues from tourism. Among the 50 states, Hawaii is the most successful in attracting visitors from Japan. Clearly, a major factor in Hawaii's success must be attributed to the travel industry and the local community's ability to understand and provide for the needs of Japanese visitors. Professor Nishiyama's research and writings have contributed to the industry's and community's efforts to serve the needs of Japanese visitors.

I believe that the real strength of *Welcoming the Japanese Visitor* lies in Professor Nishiyama's ability to combine academic expertise with years of practical experience in the tourist industry.

Prior to entering his academic career Professor Nishiyama

worked for major international airlines, hotels, and travel agencies in a managerial capacity. My association with Professor Nishiyama dates back to 1973, when he published his first book on the emerging Japanese visitor industry, *Japanese Tourists Abroad.* Since then, he has kept himself very active in research on various topics on Japan-U.S. business relationships. In 1983 he produced a series of Japanese language audiotape teaching materials, *Practical Japanese for the Tourist Industry.* In 1989 he published his second book on Japanese tourism, *Strategies of Marketing to Japanese Visitors,* and in 1993 he published a language book, *Hotel Japanese: Practical Japanese for the Hotel Industry.*

I commend Professor Nishiyama for his valuable contributions to the promotion of Japanese tourism research.

CHUCK Y. GEE
Dean, School of Travel Industry Management
University of Hawaii at Manoa

Acknowledgments

This book is the result of more than twenty years of my research studies on Japanese tourism. Since 1973 when I published my first book, *Japanese Tourists Abroad,* I have been always interested in the study of Japanese tourists' behavior, cultural influence, and economic impact on host countries. Collection of data and information for a practical book like this requires generous assistance and cooperation of many businesspeople working in the tourist industry in Japan and other countries. I have conducted many interviews in Tokyo, Hawaii, Sydney, Brisbane, Hong Kong, and Bangkok, and obtained useful information from various governmental and nongovernmental sources.

I owe a special debt of gratitude to Mr. Kenji Ito, Executive Vice President of JTB Hawaii, Inc., who made valuable introductions to his colleagues in Tokyo and Sydney, and Mr. Tsuneshige Hiroki, Assistant General Manager of JTB Hawaii, Inc., who kindly reviewed the chapter on Japanese travel companies. I wish to express my special thanks to Mr. Ichiro Matsui, Chief Analyst, Research & Data Development, Tourism Marketing Section, Japan Travel Bureau Foundation, who provided me with the most important data on Japanese tourism. I also wish to thank Mr. Tadamichi Okubo, Vice President and Regional Manager Hawaii, Japan Airlines, who provided me with valuable contacts in Tokyo, Sydney, Hong Kong, and Bangkok. I am very grateful to Mr. Hisashi Matsumoto, Senior Vice President, Kyoya Company, Ltd., who generously provided me with hotel accommodations during my research trip in Sydney. I regret that it is impossible to individually recognize many other businesspeople who directly or indirectly contributed toward the research for this book, but I would like to express my sincere appreciation for their kind assistance and generous support. I know that this book could not have been of any significance without the help of the businesspeople mentioned above.

Finally, I thank Mrs. Iris Wiley, former Executive Editor of University of Hawai'i Press, for her encouragement and guidance, and Ms. Cheri Dunn, Associate Managing Editor, and Ms. Sharon Yamamoto, Editor, for their editorial assistance.

Introduction

The spectacular increase of Japanese visitors in the past two decades has been a pleasant surprise to many businesses in tourist destinations around the world. In 1972 only 1.3 million Japanese traveled abroad, but by 1994 the number of Japanese travelers increased to 13.6 million. Despite the current economic slowdown in Japan, it is estimated that 20 million Japanese will travel overseas by the year 2000. A recent report by the Bank of Japan shows that Japanese travelers are spending more than $30 billion annually in foreign countries. The increase has been stimulated by the sharp rise in the value of the Japanese yen against major world currencies, particularly against the U.S. dollar. For example, the value of the U.S. dollar dropped from ¥300 in 1972 to ¥98 in 1994. Today more than 3.5 million Japanese visit the United States every year. Hawaii alone welcomes a total of 1.7 million visitors annually from Japan, and this number is expected to reach more than 2 million by the year 2000.

The Japanese government has been systematically and actively promoting overseas trips among its citizens and encouraging them to spend some of the large surplus of trade balance. The government has eliminated all restrictions on foreign travel and is giving a very liberal duty-free allowance for goods purchased at foreign destinations. In fact, the Ministry of Foreign Affairs now issues to its citizens multiple-entry passports that are valid for five years. Furthermore, the Japanese government has negotiated mutual visa waiver agreements with more than 51 foreign countries to allow their citizens to enter each other's country for the purpose of sightseeing, visiting relatives, and making short business trips. Japanese citizens can take an unlimited amount of foreign currency for their overseas trips. Each citizen can bring in foreign-made products totaling up to ¥200,000 or US$2,000, duty free. Other promotional measures taken by the Japanese government include conducting joint campaigns with travel-related industries to encourage Japanese workers to take longer holidays and to travel abroad, assisting public relations efforts by foreign tourism promotion organizations in Japan, providing tax incentives to encourage company recreation trips to foreign countries, promoting the use of regional airports for direct flights to and from foreign destinations, and allowing discount fares for family travel, youth, and advance-purchase tickets. The Ministry of Foreign Affairs and the Ministry of Transport are supporting the "Make Friends for Japan" campaign. This campaign is intended to make every Japanese traveler an unofficial goodwill ambassador by providing an informational booklet about Japan for the peoples of host countries. The booklet includes such topics as family life, work life, education, housing, seasonal festivals, weddings, and simple Japanese games. It also includes advice to Japanese travelers on etiquette and proper behavior in foreign countries.

With the Japanese government's positive attitude toward foreign travel and the extremely active tour promotions by Japan's huge travel industry, Japanese visitor spending will continue to be a very important factor in world economics. For those countries with a large trade deficit with Japan, this visitor spending has been an important "intangible export" to Japan, which will help reduce the trade deficit. Japanese visitors are welcomed by tourism-oriented countries around the world because they are big spenders: They still spend a large amount of money on souvenirs *(omiyage)*, they eat at fine restaurants, and they stay at luxury hotels. Honeymooners often spend thousands of dollars on gifts for relatives and friends and pay for deluxe hotel accommodations, limousine service, and fine cuisine. Unmarried female office workers tend to buy expensive brand-name items from specialty shops. Businessmen entertain their clients with golf games and fine dining, and they often give expensive gifts to maintain good business relationships. More affluent families now spend their vacations at foreign resorts on a regular basis. Even student groups have begun to travel to foreign countries for both educational and recreational purposes.

If businesses in host countries wish to reap the benefits of Japanese visitor spending, they must understand the unique travel habits and preferences of the Japanese and must make a special effort to provide good products and services to them. Businesses must also understand that Japanese visitors are no longer innocent and gullible tourists. Japanese travelers have a fairly good knowledge about foreign destinations through their own travel experience, the mass media, guidebooks, and tour brochures written in Japanese. They do expect good value for the money they spend.

This book was written for businesspeople in tourism-related industries and anyone interested in learning about the Japanese visitor market and the proper way of doing business with Japanese travel companies. Part I, Understanding Japanese Visitors, covers the reasons for Japanese travel overseas; the visitor attractions, sports, and other activities preferred by Japanese visitors; the profile and market segmentation of the Japanese visitor market; and the media promotion and other promotion strategies of travel products. Part II, Catering to Japanese Visitors, covers hotel and food and beverage service for Japanese visitors, the shopping habits of Japanese visitors and effective souvenir merchandising, air transportation and local sightseeing tours, and proper nonverbal communication with Japanese customers. Part III, Doing Businesses with Japanese Travel Companies, covers Japanese travel agencies and their tour products, effective ways of initiating and maintaining business contacts, and the proper methods of contract negotiation and dispute resolution. The appendixes include a glossary of Japanese terms, a list of the top twenty Japanese tour wholesalers, and a list of international tourism organizations in Japan.

It is my sincere hope that this book will be of value to those businesspeople who wish to cultivate and maintain business relations with Japanese travel companies and to those college students who are majoring in travel industry management, international marketing, and intercultural communication. I believe that it will also be a valuable reference to human resources managers and management consultants responsible for training hotel personnel, restaurant workers, retail store salespersons, and others in tourism-related businesses.

PART I

UNDERSTANDING

JAPANESE VISITORS

Despite the economic benefits of serving Japanese visitors, most businesses in host countries are not well prepared to reap the benefits of the huge amount of Japanese visitor spending. Many foreign businesspeople in the tourist industry, out of frustration, accuse Japanese-owned businesses of developing a closed system. One of the most frequent complaints in local newspapers is that Japanese tourists fly Japan Airlines and use Japanese-owned hotels, buses, souvenir shops, restaurants, and golf courses. There is some validity to this complaint, but the simple truth is that most businesses do not understand Japanese visitors and their behavior. Japanese visitors are very different from their English-speaking counterparts from the United States, Canada, Australia, and European countries. The Japanese have different reasons for traveling overseas and have different expectations and preferences. They like to take sightseeing tours to famous tourist destinations to satisfy their curiosity and also go shopping and engage in outdoor sports activities. The Japanese, in general, are not experienced overseas travelers and still travel in groups. They are not as flexible and adaptable as other foreign visitors might be. In recent years, they have been the targets of intensive marketing efforts by various businesses in the visitor industry of major tourism-oriented countries from all over the world. Japanese travelers are well informed about overseas destinations and tour packages through a wide variety of communication media available to them. In order to gain a good share of the Japanese overseas travel market, it is important to understand the Japanese visitors' travel habits, favorite visitor attractions, market segmentation, promotion media, and other effective promotion strategies.

Chapter 1

Reasons for Overseas Travel

Japanese people have always found much enjoyment and excitement in traveling. Indeed, they are habitual travelers at home as they can easily find a variety of places to visit within Japan. Many Japanese take two or three short overnight trips a year.[1] To them, traveling to foreign countries is a natural extension, and one that they can readily enjoy. They also prefer to travel in groups whenever they visit foreign destinations.

Strong Interests in Traveling

Japan is one of the most beautiful countries in East Asia, with hundreds of scenic spots, historical sites, and cultural attractions. There are many picturesque mountains, lakes, waterfalls, rivers, beaches, and hot-spring resorts. Japan is a chain of verdant islands off the east coast of the huge continental land mass of China and the Korean Peninsula. These islands are surrounded by the vast sweep of the Pacific Ocean on the east and the Sea of Japan on the west. The Japanese archipelago contains a great variety of topographical features, with several high volcanic mountain ranges. Extending from the northern island of Hokkaido to the southern island of Kyushu, Japan has distinct contrasts in climate and rich seasonal changes by regions. Consequently, the Japanese have developed a keen appreciation for the beauties of nature and the different seasons.

Japan also contains ancient Shinto shrines and Buddhist temples, famous national parks and museums, and other natural treasures that they can visit. Traditionally, the Japanese begin the new year by visiting Shinto shrines. During the first five days of the new year, Japanese businesspeople visit famous shrines to pray for a prosperous new year. Men wear new business suits, and women wear colorful kimonos for this occasion. They also call on their relatives and friends at their homes. Millions of those Japanese who work in large cities return to their own native towns and villages in the countryside during the New Year holidays.

From early to late spring the Japanese travel far to view, in seasonal order, plum blossom and cherry blossom in parks, azalea bushes in full bloom on hillsides, and iris flowers in the shallows of lakes. Cherry blossom viewing *(ohanami)* is the most popular springtime event for the Japanese. Every spring, thousands of people picnic under the blooming cherry trees and enjoy drinking, eating, singing, dancing, and merrymaking.

In summer, the Japanese flock to mountain resorts to escape from the hot weather and to the beaches for swimming. In autumn, they seek out the colorful autumn leaves and enjoy the bountiful harvest from the land and sea. In winter, young Japanese and the young at heart go to ski resorts in the Japan Alps and on the northern island of Hokkaido. Hot-spring resorts also enjoy brisk business during autumn and winter seasons. Kyoto, the ancient capital of Japan, with many old temples, attracts tens of thousands of visitors throughout the year. Kinkakuji (Gold Pavilion), Kiyomizu Temple, and Ryoanji Temple are the most famous national treasures.

During every season, regional festivals attract visitors from all over the country. These festivals reflect ancient religious beliefs, folk tales, and the traditional customs of each locality. The Star Festival *(Tanabata)*, held in Sendai on July 7, is the most famous in Japan. This festival traces its origin to the legend that the constellations of Vega and Altair meet once a year. In celebration, people write down their wishes on strips of paper, which they then hang from bamboo branches. Merchants in those cities make and display large decorative lanterns with long colorful streamers on long bamboo poles. In the summer months large-scale fireworks displays light up the skies to the delight of the spectators. During harvesttime in early fall, townspeople and villagers celebrate autumn festivals by carrying heavy portable shrines *(mikoshi)* of Shinto gods through the streets. It is believed that the more booming their shouts, the bigger the next harvest will be. These festivals attract a very large number of visitors from neighboring cities and towns.

Japanese literature is full of travelogues describing the natural beauty, unique foods and products, and unusual customs of different regions. During the Meiji Restoration (1868–1911), Japan borrowed so much from the West. In its effort to catch up with the more advanced Western nations, the Japanese government imported Western literature, art, fashion, medicine, philosophy, political thought, the judicial system, education, industrial technology, military science, and commerce. As a consequence, Japanese people have always been interested in visiting the Western countries from which they learned so many things. Since the end of World War II, the influence of the United States has been particularly strong in Japan. American movies, pop music, popular magazines, casual wear, cosmetics, fast foods, and soft drinks have inundated Japan in recent years. The American youth culture has instilled a great curiosity about the United States among young Japanese.

Information about overseas tourist destinations is disseminated widely through extensive Japanese television coverage. A wide variety of travelogues, sports programs, and documentary films from many parts of the world are available to the average Japanese right in his own living room. Today, satellite communications bring instant coverage of world events from every corner of the globe to Japanese television viewers, with simultaneous translation or Japanese subtitles. Many Japanese wish to travel overseas to confirm what they have read about or seen on television.

Changes in Work Culture and Leisure Boom

Japanese people have long been considered workaholics. Compared to the people of other industrialized Western nations, they still seem to work much harder. A recent survey by the Japanese Ministry of Labor estimates that Japanese work an average of 2,190 hours a year, Americans 1,920 hours, British 1,890 hours, French 1,683 hours, and Germans 1,598 hours.[2] Recognizing this situation, the Japanese government has begun promoting a five-day work week, full use of paid annual vacation, long week-ends, and a shortening of working hours. Consequently, almost all of the Japanese government offices and large private enter-prises have a five-day work week, although many small compa-nies still practice a six-day work week. Other smaller companies allow Saturdays off once or twice a month. The average Japanese worker is actually entitled to 15.5 days of annual vacation, but most of them take only 8.2 days, or 52.7 percent.[3] They are still reluctant to use the entire vacation time due to the social pres-sure exerted by their superiors and fellow workers. If workers take a two-week vacation, they worry that they will be ostracized not only for being disloyal, but also for being selfish. For this rea-son, a "good" Japanese worker will take only three or four days of his vacation time and combine it with a long holiday weekend when he goes on an overseas vacation. If he really wants to take the two-week vacation to which he is legally entitled, he may have to worry about being fired. Recent research by the Japan Travel Bureau Foundation shows that 14.5 percent of Japanese workers took one to four days for their travel, 39 percent took five to seven days, 37.4 percent took eight to fourteen days, and only 9.1 percent took fifteen days or more. The research also shows that shorter trips to closer destinations are the most popular among Japanese travelers. Of trips to Korea, Hong Kong, Tai-wan, and Macau, 56 percent are four days or less, and 42.2 per-cent of trips to Guam and Saipan are less than four days. Even trips to Latin America, the Middle East, and Africa are between five and seven days. In fact, the trend is for workers to take vaca-tions of shorter duration to distant destinations, even though the share of trips of eight to fourteen days long has been slowly increasing every year.[4]

On the other hand, today's new breed of young Japanese (*shinjinrui*) do not have the same serious work attitude as the older generation. An increasing number of young Japanese work-ers are adopting the leisure habits long taken for granted by workers in industrialized Western countries. Young Japanese workers are more inclined to take longer vacations without feel-ing guilty. They do not volunteer to work overtime on weekends and prefer not to socialize exclusively with coworkers. Today there are many young Japanese women and some young men who do not seek lifetime careers with one company and prefer to work on a project as temporary workers. The current fad among young Japanese women is to work on a six-month or one-year project, take a few months off between jobs, and then take an extended overseas trip. A recent development is the use of the "working holidays system" by young Japanese who wish to spend a long holiday in a foreign country. Currently, Japan has a mutual agreement with Australia, New Zealand, and Canada allowing young adults (18 to 25 years of age) to have one-year working holidays in one of these participating countries. The major objective of this system is to promote mutual understanding and goodwill between participants and the host nationals through face-to-face contact in work situations.[5] If these trends continue, more and more young Japanese will be taking longer overseas vacations in the near future.

Friends and Relatives Living Overseas

Today approximately 250,000 Japanese are living in foreign countries as businessmen, diplomats, scholars and researchers, and students. If a few thousand Japanese nationals are living in one foreign city or town, there will be "Japanese-only associations" such as the Japanese chamber of commerce, Japanese businessmen's clubs, Japanese amateur golf associations, Japanese women's clubs, Japanese prefecture clubs, and Japanese schools. There are also many Japanese martial arts schools (judo, kendo, karate, aikido) and Japanese culture schools (flower arrangement, tea ceremony, dancing, and singing) that are branches of their Japan headquarters. The Japanese language television and radio programs, Japanese newspapers, Japanese books, and Japanese magazines that are available in these communities make Japanese visitors feel at home. Indeed, there are many well-established Japanese communities in most major cities of the United States, Australia, Canada, and Europe. These overseas Japanese encourage their friends and relatives to visit them while they are living there. Such invitations are a strong motivator for many Japanese people, because most of them prefer to travel to places where they can find Japanese-speaking friends and relatives. These people can be their friends' friends or distant relatives, but they still find psychological comfort knowing that they can depend on those people for advice and assistance. In fact, those Japanese who live in major tourist destinations such as Hawaii, San Francisco, Los Angeles, Chicago, New York, Washington, D.C., London, Frankfurt, Copenhagen, Bangkok, Hong Kong, Korea, Singapore, or the Gold Coast in Australia complain that they have to act as tour guides and hosts to visiting friends and relatives too often. One of the major reasons Hawaii is still the most popular destination even today is that it is a very comfortable destination for Japanese visitors. Some Japanese travel experts say that Hawaii has become one of the "domestic destinations" for repeat visitors from Japan. Today about 40 percent of Japanese visitors to Hawaii are repeaters. The recent popularity of Hawaii-born sumo champions Akebono, Konishiki, and Musashimaru has made Hawaii even more familiar to the entire population of Japan. A sense of familiarity and affinity with the local Japanese population seems to be quite important in attracting visitors from Japan.

In addition, those Japanese who have returned to Japan from foreign sojourns enthusiastically talk about their wonderful experiences. These souvenir stories *(miyagebanashi)* by returnees also encourage their friends and relatives to visit that particular city or country and see for themselves what the returnees have experienced. In many cases, Japanese visitors seek the friends of the returnees who are still living there, and ask for assistance. Personal contacts are still a very important reason for Japanese who plan to travel overseas. A survey by the information bureau of the prime minister's office of Japan supports the importance of influence by friends and relatives. It shows that the two top-ranked reasons they traveled were (1) they were "encouraged by friends and acquaintances" and (2) "prompted by family members."[6] This particular motivation to travel is substantiated by other research by the Japan Travel Bureau Foundation. It reports that 33 percent of males and 14.3 percent of females between the ages of 15 and 19 traveled overseas for the purpose of visiting relatives and friends. Likewise, about 10 percent of women in the 40 to 49, 50 to 59, and 60 or older age groups went abroad for this purpose.[7]

Getting Away from Congestion

Japan is one of the most densely populated countries in the world. Its total land size is 145,875 square miles (377,815 square kilometers), which is slightly smaller than the state of California, or about one-twenty-fifth of the United States. This figure includes the four main islands of Hokkaido, Honshu, Shikoku, and Kyushu and roughly 3,000 smaller islands that stretch about 1,860 miles (2,993 kilometers) from north to south. Japan has a great variety of topographical features because it consists of several high volcanic ranges throughout the country. About 70 percent of Japan's islands are mountainous, and less than 20 percent of the land can be used for agriculture. Only 5 percent of the land area is suitable for residential use, and a mere 4 percent is devoted to industrial use. Despite this small land area, Japan's population in 1994 was about 125,000,000—almost one-half the population of the United States and much larger than the populations of Germany and Britain.[8] And the distribution of Japan's population is uneven: about 70 percent of the entire population lives on the strip of coastal plains between the northern part of Kyushu and of Honshu, where the weather is mild and where major cities and industries are located. In Japan the population density is about 800 persons per square mile, but large metropolitan areas have a much higher density. For example, Tokyo has almost 12,000,000 people living in an area of 836 square miles (14,181 persons per square mile). Osaka has more than 8,734,670 persons in an area of 722 square miles (12,098 persons per square mile), and Yokohama has more than 7,980,421 persons in an area of 928 square miles (8,600 persons per square mile). These metropolitan areas do not have enough parks, athletic fields, sports facilities, and open spaces for such large populations. Obviously, the people who live in these congested metropolitan areas must get away to foreign countries, where they can find open spaces and natural beauty. A recent survey by the Ministry of Justice and Ministry of Home Affairs shows that almost 20 percent of Tokyo residents and 15 percent of Yokohama residents went abroad, whereas only 9.5 percent of the residents of less populated areas went abroad.[9]

Financial Incentives for Overseas Travel

Today, due to the rapid economic growth of recent years, a much larger proportion of the Japanese population has enough money to travel overseas. The average income of the Japanese worker has increased substantially in recent years, and it is now approximately equal to that of workers in the United States and Germany. The recent rise in the value of the Japanese yen against major world currencies, particularly against the U.S. dollar, has made overseas trips a bargain for Japanese visitors. The yen has appreciated more than 40 percent over the past four years. The exchange rate against one U.S. dollar was ¥145 in 1990, ¥135 in 1991, ¥127 in 1992, and ¥110 in 1993. But in the summer of 1994 the value shot up to ¥98 per U.S. dollar. Consequently, trips to tourist destinations in the United States became bargains for Japanese visitors. And trips to other overseas destinations have become much less expensive than domestic sightseeing trips due to the strong yen against other foreign currencies. Today, the Japanese can truly enjoy value for their money when traveling abroad.

Japan's unique bonus system also provides extra money for travel. Japanese corporations, national and regional governments, and public and private educational institutions pay bonuses twice a year, usually in June and December. Although the amount of the bonus fluctuates somewhat, the total is between 40 and 50 percent of the annual base salary. For example, a young Japanese worker may receive an annual salary of $24,000, or $2,000 a month. If he receives a bonus of 50 percent of his annual wage, he will be paid an additional 25 percent ($6,000) in June and another 25 percent in December. His total income then becomes $36,000 instead of $24,000. If he is thrifty and lives on his $2,000 monthly wage, he can use the $12,000 bonus for overseas travel. Besides this liberal bonus system, Japanese companies provide several fringe benefits such as housing allowances, commuting allowances, lunch subsidies, and family allowances.

It is important to know that many Japanese do not finance their overseas trips entirely themselves; family members, employers, and friends help by giving customary monetary gifts to those relatives, friends, and fellow workers going on long trips. Many companies offer "bonus trips" to those employees with many years of continuous service as an incentive reward. Incentive trips are always paid for in full by the sponsoring company. According to a survey by the Japan Travel Bureau Foundation, about 60 percent of travelers paid for all of their travel costs by themselves, about 25 percent received a full subsidy from their employers or other sponsoring organizations, and about 15 percent received a partial subsidy from their employers or other organizations. Interestingly, 41.3 percent of married men and 40 percent of the middle-aged group were given free trips. On the other hand, only 9.2 percent of young working women and 15.6 percent of older working women received free trips.[10] Japanese companies usually sponsor company recreation trips, incentive tours, and overseas study tours or trade-fair attendance.

Various travel savings plans are also very popular methods of financing excursions. For school excursions, school administrations encourage each class to start a savings plan at the beginning of the school year. The class treasurer collects a set amount of money from each classmate every month and deposits it in a local bank. When the time of the annual excursion approaches, every student will have enough to pay for the trip. Retail merchant associations may have their own travel savings plan for those members who wish to visit a specific foreign tourist destination on the association-sponsored group tour. They may have a three-year savings plan for a Hawaiian vacation and a five-year savings plan for a European vacation. Many Japanese banks and major tour wholesalers offer travel loans and issue credit cards to their customers. Today, many Japanese do not hesitate to take out loans for overseas travel, although some Japanese still feel uncomfortable about borrowing money for pleasure trips.

Traveling as Group Members

Japanese visitors are well known as group travelers, and this holds true even when they travel to overseas destinations. Japanese travelers are not as independent and adventurous as Americans or Europeans and are reluctant to venture out on their own.

Japanese people become accustomed to group travel very early in life. From kindergarten through high school, students are required to go on annual school excursions *(shuugaku ryokoo)*. School administrations usually arrange transportation, lodging, meals, sightseeing stops, and cultural spots to visit for these excursions. Each grade level goes on the excursion together escorted by teachers in charge. On each trip, they visit some of Japan's national monuments, national treasures, museums, famous shrines and temples, scenic spots, modern high-tech factories, government buildings, and office towers. The Japanese Ministry of Education provides guidance on the planning and execution of every school excursion. The ministry also provides partial financial assistance to children from economically disadvantaged families, since the excursions are considered an integral part of formal education and an important social experience. The students are able to actually see and experience firsthand what they have learned in the classrooms. They also experience "group living" and learn how to get along with each other by spending a few days and nights together. The students are required to submit a written report on their experience within a few weeks of the trip. One-day excursions are usually reserved for kindergarten and younger elementary school children. Two- to five-day excursions are common among junior high school and senior high school students. Consequently, Japanese students will have visited many famous tourist destinations within Japan by the time they finish their formal education, and they will have also become experienced group travelers.

When these students graduate from school and start working, this group travel is perpetuated by company recreation trips *(ian ryokoo)*. Japanese companies sponsor and pay for (in part or in whole) annual excursions to famous tourist destinations. These trips are tax-deductible expenses because they are considered employee health and welfare expenditures. The real purpose of these company-sponsored recreation trips is to facilitate communication and to promote goodwill between company management and employees. In addition to the company-wide recreation trips, departments or sections within the company usually sponsor short excursions for smaller groups.

Incentive tours *(shootai ryokoo)* sponsored by Japanese manufacturers and wholesalers also provide many opportunities for retail merchants to travel in groups. Since business is done through direct personal contacts in Japan, these incentive tours are an invaluable means of promoting goodwill and loyalty among the clients of these sponsoring companies. Besides these group tours, other affinity groups such as farmers cooperatives and shopping center tenants associations sponsor a variety of discount group tours. For example, the Japan Farmers Cooperatives (Nokyoo) offer to its members a large number of group tours. The retail merchants' association of the Sunshine Building Shopping Arcade may sponsor an annual trip to a foreign country that combines field studies and recreation.

Japanese people prefer to travel in groups for both cultural and practical reasons:(1) International airlines offer special air fares based on block-booking or annual sales volume to tour wholesalers. Likewise, hotels and sightseeing tour companies give substantial discounts to tour wholesalers. The wholsealers, in turn, offer reasonably priced tour packages to the traveling public. For them, it is not practical to buy tickets, book hotel rooms, and arrange ground transportation on their own because it would cost much more. Group discount *(dantai waribiki)* is applicable to foreign travel except in high peak seasons. (2) The Japanese find a sense of comfort *(anshin kan)* in traveling with other Japanese, especially when traveling overseas. Even though an increasing number of Japanese speak some English, they are rather shy and hesitate to interact with foreigners on their own. They also find that travel agents and tour escorts provide a much better service to larger groups than to individuals. (3) Still another incentive for group travel is that travelers can join a variety of Japanese-speaking group tours to anywhere in the world. Traditionally, group tours meant that travelers had to be bona fide members of a certain affinity group, association, corporation, or institution. But today, anyone can join these package tours organized by Japanese tour wholesalers. For example, a honeymoon couple from Tokyo can join one of those Hawaiian honeymoon package tours with twenty other pairs of honeymooners from other cities. Two young office workers can choose to join an economy tour to Hong Kong at a few days' notice. In other words, they travel as group members with fifty other individual travelers whom they have never met before just to take advantage of discount air fares and inexpensive hotel accommodations.

In recent years, more and more young repeat travelers have joined tour groups for this reason. And once these travelers reach their destinations, they plan and execute their own sightseeing, shopping, and sports activities rather than go along with other tour members.

Chapter 2

Visitor Attractions and Sports Activities

The visitor attractions and sports activities at foreign destinations chosen by Japanese visitors are largely influenced by what they are used to doing in Japan and by their curiosity to experience something new and exotic. The choices may also differ by the destination and by their demographic backgrounds, such as age, sex, marital status, income, and occupation. Several of the most popular attractions and tour activities are nature and scenery, historical sites and famous architecture, art galleries and museums, amusement parks and entertainments, outdoor sports, rest and recreation, gambling, and romantic encounters.

Nature and Scenery

Sightseeing *(kankoo)* in Japanese literally means "viewing of natural scenery." From early childhood, Japanese people have learned to appreciate the beautiful nature and sceneries abundant in their own country through frequent family trips, school excursions, and company recreation trips. Consequently, those famous scenic spots and the natural beauty in foreign countries are the most popular attractions for Japanese visitors. The visitors actually have a list of must-see places and are disappointed if they are unable to go there. Tour wholesalers and local tour operators always make certain that the most famous scenic spots and landmarks at every destination are covered in all package tour itineraries. Japanese visitors like to take *kinen shashin* (souvenir photos) to show that they have been to those places. For this purpose there are fairly large picture-taking stands with three or four steps for group-picture taking at almost all of the most famous landmarks in Japan.

Japanese travelers visit those scenic spots that are popularized by tour brochures, guidebooks, and promotional films. For example, visitors to the island of Oahu, in Hawaii, never fail to visit Waikiki Beach, Diamond Head, Hanauma Bay, and Nuuanu Pali. Visitors to the West Coast of the United States visit the Golden Gate Bridge, Nob Hill, Muir Woods National Park, and Yosemite National Park in California, and Grand Canyon National Park in Arizona. And visitors to Australia see Sydney Harbor, the Opera House, the Great Barrier Reef, and Ayers Rock. In addition to the scenic sites, Japanese visitors are very interested in the ancient legends and fables associated with each of these places and in buying such mementos as postcards, booklets, and small souvenir items.

Recently, many Japanese civic organizations and certain individuals have begun to pay attention to the conservation of nature. Today it has become fashionable for them to join special tours designed for viewing wildflowers and plants, wildlife in its natural habitat, and for tree planting. This "ecotourism" is a new attraction for ecology-minded Japanese visitors.

Historical Sites and Famous Architecture

In Japan, there are many ancient Shinto shrines, Buddhist temples, castles, and other historic buildings that are considered national treasures. These places are always included in domestic sightseeing trips because the Japanese are generally very interested in history, and this is why they like to visit historic sites and famous architecture at tourist destinations in foreign countries. They will be particularly interested in going to those places they have seen on television programs and read about in books. For example, Japanese visitors to the East Coast of the United States visit Capitol Hill, the White House, the Lincoln Memorial, and the Washington Monument in Washington, D.C., and the Statue of Liberty, the Empire State Building, and Broadway in New York City. When the Japanese travel to Europe, they visit the Vatican,

Fountain of Piazza, Sistine Chapel, Trevi Fountain, and Colosseum in Rome, and the Eiffel Tower, Notre Dame Cathedral, Palace of Versailles, and Arc de Triomphe in Paris.

Because of their interest in history, Japanese travelers also like visiting art galleries and museums. Indeed, almost all Japanese visitors are interested in visiting world-famous art galleries and museums at overseas destinations because visits to art galleries and museums are important features of school excursions and sightseeing trips in Japan. Older Japanese visitors with a post-secondary education in particular seem to enjoy visiting these places when traveling abroad.

Amusement Parks and Entertainment

Since Japan does not have enough public parks for its residents, they need to visit private amusement parks. There are many amusement parks in every large population center. Some of these parks are replicas of famous American and European amusement parks. One of the most successful parks is Tokyo Disneyland, which has the highest attendance every year among all the amusement parks in the world. Obviously, Japanese visitors' interest in amusement parks has been influenced by its tremendous popularity. Many young visitors may have been there while still in school, either on their school excursion or on a family vacation trip. Naturally, when these visitors go to the United States, they will want to visit Disneyland in Anaheim, California, Universal Studios in Los Angeles, and Walt Disney World in Orlando, Florida. And when they go to the Gold Coast of Brisbane, Australia, they will want to see Dreamworld.

Japanese visitors are also interested in visiting zoos, sea-life parks, aquariums, and botanical gardens. Honeymoon couples, young female office workers, and families with small children certainly seem to enjoy visiting these huge parks and exhibits.

The Japanese are generally curious and inquisitive people. They have always been interested in learning about regional ethnic cultures through folk songs and folk dances. When they visit Hawaii they almost always go to Hawaiian shows to see hula dancers, and when they go to Alaska they want to see Eskimo dancing.

The Japanese are also interested in meeting and talking with the indigenous people of the particular localities.

Japanese visitors are also interested in the nightclub shows of world-famous entertainers. For example, shows by Michael Jackson and Madonna are considered good attractions. Other variations are shows by popular Japanese entertainers held at popular overseas tourist destinations. For example, a famous Japanese singer might come to Hawaii with his fan club members and hold a special show, perhaps called "A Hawaiian Evening with the Star." In a case like this, a large number of fan club members from Japan and from Hawaii will attend this entertainer's show. This is a smart marketing idea that can attract a large group of Japanese visitors during a slow tourist season.

Many Japanese like Western music and musicals. Japanese entertainment promoters often invite famous symphony groups, jazz bands, opera companies, and ballet troupes from foreign countries. Seeing these performances makes Japanese visitors want to see the same musical event in the country of origin. For example, they may want to attend a performance by the London Philharmonic Orchestra while visiting London, or they may want to attend jazz concerts while in New Orleans.

Outdoor Sports

Japanese visitors are very interested in outdoor sports and recreation, as many of them are not able to enjoy these pastimes in Japan due to physical and financial constraints. The most popular outdoor sports activities are golf, tennis, marathons, fishing, swimming, snorkeling, scuba diving, jet skiing, parasailing, yachting, motorboating, and skiing.

Golf

Golfing is the most popular sport among the Japanese. It is estimated that approximately 10 million Japanese play golf, but there are only 2,000 golf courses in Japan. This shortage of golf courses not only makes it difficult for golfers to get a tee time, but it also makes golfing very expensive. Prestigious private club memberships are reserved for wealthy individuals and large corporations, as the members usually need to pay from several hundred thousand to more than one million dollars for a membership. (In Japan golf club memberships are transferable to others and can be bought and sold like stock certificates.) Ordinarily, Japanese golfers living in large cities must travel two to three hours one way to get to the golf course in the countryside, and they pay between $300 and $500 for a round of golf. Consequently, Japanese visitors find golfing at foreign destinations very attractive and much more enjoyable.

Japanese tour wholesalers and local tour operators are very successful at selling golfing as an optional tour. To make good profits from golf tours sold to Japanese visitors, many Japanese real estate developers have built or purchased golf courses in Hawaii, California, Guam, Saipan, Australia, and other popular golf destinations. Some of these companies also sell nonresident golf club memberships to golf enthusiasts in Japan. The members are provided with preferential tee times and other personalized services by Japanese-speaking staff. In addition, Japanese-owned resort hotels have their own golf courses for the convenience of guests who want to play golf while staying there. Japanese tour wholesalers and local tour operators have special arrangements with these golf clubs so that they can sell golf tours to their clients with guaranteed tee times on a daily basis.

Tennis

Tennis has become a very popular sport among the Japanese, especially among young office workers and high school and college students. Major corporations sponsor company tennis teams, and private athletic clubs promote tennis games among the affluent Japanese. Both private and public schools have tennis teams and hold annual interscholastic tennis tournaments. Some Japanese high schools send their tennis teams to foreign countries for goodwill tournaments. The increasing popularity of tennis is fanned by the publicity of a few seeded Japanese professional tennis players on the world tours who compete against the world's top-seeded players.

Despite the popularity of tennis, the number of existing tennis courts in the metropolitan areas of Japan cannot accommodate all of the tennis enthusiasts. As with golf clubs, private tennis club memberships are very expensive. For most of the tennis players, finding a tennis court is a difficult and frustrating experience. During the months of December, January, and February, and during the rainy season of June and July, it becomes even more difficult for them to play tennis outdoors. Consequently, playing tennis at tropical or subtropical foreign destinations is a big treat for Japanese visitors who play tennis. Many of these tennis players bring their favorite tennis rackets with them when they travel overseas.

Marathons

Long-distance running is one of the few sports that Japan has excelled at in the Olympics. Every year many different Japanese organizations sponsor marathons, and tens of thousands of runners participate. Today a new trend among Japanese runners is to participate in international marathon events, which are aggressively promoted by tour wholesalers and airlines. For example, the annual Honolulu Marathon, sponsored by Japan Airlines, has become one of the biggest Japanese visitor attractions in Hawaii. More than ten thousand amateur runners and a few professionals run a twenty-six-mile course against American and other foreign participants on the second Sunday of December every year. For the majority of Japanese runners, this is a boisterous sports festival rather than an athletic meet. The marathon is intentionally scheduled in December, the slowest time of Hawaii's tourist season, in order to boost airline, hotel, restaurant, and retail business. In recent years it has become a truly international event, and several Japanese television stations broadcast it live in Japan.

Fishing

Fishing is one of the most popular pastimes for many Japanese. They go to rivers and streams for fly-fishing and go to coastal waters on launches and boats for ocean fishing during specific fishing seasons. Many Japanese visitors who enjoy fishing may go to Hawaii, Guam, Saipan, the Gulf of Mexico, and the Great Barrier Reef for deep-sea fishing. For example, Kona, on the island of Hawaii, has been extremely successful in attracting Japanese fishing enthusiasts. Kona is well known among the Japanese because of the publicity generated by the annual International Billfish

Tournament held every August. This tournament attracts several Japanese fishing teams who compete against other international teams in catching huge Pacific blue marlins.

Water Sports

Swimming, snorkeling, scuba diving, jet skiing, parasailing, surfing, windsurfing, and yachting are favorite sports for almost all Japanese. In Japan, they can engage in many of these water sports only during the warm summer months of July and August. *Kaisui-yoku* (ocean water bathing) is the most popular summer pastime for Japanese families with young children. Tens of thousands of swimmers flock to the beaches of coastal towns during summer weekends. The beaches near the Tokyo and Yokohama metropolitan areas become so congested that it appears as though the swimmers are moving about in a large Jacuzzi tub. Swimming pools in amusement parks are just as full of people on holidays and weekends. The congestion at the beaches is also due to the fact that only a few of Japan's coastal areas are safe for water sports because of strong currents and lower water temperatures. This is the reason why Japanese visitors want to engage in water sports on the tropical islands of the Pacific and the Caribbean. According to a recent survey, 70 percent of travelers who visited Hawaii, 55 percent of those who visited Guam, and 36 percent of those who visited Tahiti engaged in water activities.[1]

Scuba diving is considered a young person's sport. Today many young Japanese have taken up the sport and enjoy diving in warm tropical seas. Some Japanese visitors take classes on scuba diving and obtain licenses in foreign countries because the licensing course is very expensive in Japan. There are optional tour packages for scuba diving marketed by Japanese tour operators. Jet skiing and parasailing are other popular water sports for young Japanese visitors. These are thrilling experiences and require little training and preparation.

Surfing and windsurfing have become extremely popular among some young Japanese men, and there are many surfing and windsurfing clubs. Since Japan's weather is not always conducive to safe surfing, many of the professional surfers and windsurfers go to Hawaii, California, and Australia to train for international meets. A small number of inexperienced Japanese visitors may try surfing and windsurfing to satisfy their curiosity when they go to tropical island destinations.

Yachting is a recent craze among affluent Japanese individuals. Many of them own yachts and motorboats. Several Japanese yachting teams even compete in international yacht races such as the World Cup in San Diego and the Kenwood Cup in Hawaii. However, there are only 42 public marinas with some 11,386 berths in Japan to accommodate 54,000 yachts and 280,000 motorboats.[2] This certainly creates difficulties for the operation and mooring of pleasure boats. Chartered yachts and motorboats, then, can be a very strong incentive for Japanese boaters to visit destinations where they can enjoy boating. In fact, Hawaii, Guam, Saipan, Thailand, Malaysia, Tahiti, and Australia attract a large number of Japanese yachters and pleasure boaters every year.

Skiing

Skiing is the most popular winter sport in Japan. Japanese skiers have attained world-class performance levels, particularly in long-jump competitions. Japan will be hosting the Winter Olympics in Nagano in 1998. Despite the bursting of Japan's "bubble economy" in 1991, a recent survey shows the tremendous popularity of skiing among the Japanese. This means that skiers from all over Japan flock to Japan's ski resorts in large numbers during the winter ski season, and they must cope with very congested conditions when they go skiing. To capitalize on this situation, Japanese tour wholesalers offer ski tours to Colorado, Anchorage, Alaska, the Canadian Rockies, and New Zealand. Several Japanese corporations have even purchased ski resorts and work with tour wholesalers to promote overseas ski trips. Today more and more young Japanese get away from Japan during the New Year's holiday and go to foreign ski resorts for skiing. One major tour wholesaler offers a package tour that includes skiing, snowmobiling, horse-drawn sled riding, and ice fishing. This company also offers a European ski honeymoon tour to Switzerland for newlyweds.

The popularity of skiing among young residents of large cities around Tokyo prompted the building of two ski domes in nearby Chiba. The indoor ski slopes with artificial snow do very good business. Many commuters to Tokyo and nearby residents go there after work and on weekends, as these facilities are open year round for ski enthusiasts.

Rest and Recreation

From ancient times, the Japanese have made frequent trips to hot-spring resorts to bathe in natural hot spring waters because they believe that the waters contain minerals for the healing of physical ailments and other sicknesses. For many Japanese, rest and recreation often mean taking an overnight trip to a hot-spring resort. Such a trip typically includes good meals, local sightseeing, and perhaps a round of golf. It always provides both physical relief and mental relaxation.

Now that package tours have become affordable, a large number of Japanese go to overseas destinations for rest and recreation. A recent survey by a semigovernmental agency reports that an overseas trip was ranked 4th among the 20 most desirable leisure activities. The same survey shows an attitudinal change in the average Japanese worker: 24.5 percent of the people surveyed said, "I finish my work as efficiently as possible, and enjoy my leisure time"; 26 percent said, "I find leisure and work equally important"; 35 percent said, "I enjoy my leisure time, but I work hard as well"; and 4 percent said, "I find my work most challenging and devote myself toward it."[3] This survey clearly indicates that the current generation of Japanese workers wants to have more time for rest and recreation. They are no longer true workaholics or economic animals, as they were so often labeled by foreign observers in the past.

As mentioned earlier, all Japanese government offices have initiated the five-day work week. Likewise, almost all larger companies have begun cutting down working hours. In the past few years, a substantial number of corporations began encouraging their officers and employees to take more holidays for rest and relaxation due to slowdowns in many sectors of the Japanese economy.

In response to this growing trend in rest and recreation, Japanese real estate developers have built deluxe hotels and condominiums with golf courses, tennis courts, swimming pools, and health spas at many world-famous resort destinations. They sell corporate memberships to Japanese companies. Large corporations have even built their own corporate retreats in popular foreign resort towns and villages. For example, Nomura Securities, Nintendo, and Toyota Motors have built plush resort complexes in Hawaii.

More affluent Japanese have begun traveling for health and recuperation. Those people suffering from health problems go to suitable foreign destinations for recuperation, if they can find proper medical care there. For example, Hawaii has become one of the most popular places for these Japanese visitors because it has several hospitals with Japanese-speaking physicians and nurses. Hawaii has clear skies, clean air, good water, and a mild climate year round, and more importantly, it has many good Japanese restaurants and several supermarkets that carry a wide variety of Japanese foods.

Gambling and Romantic Encounters

The Japanese government does not allow casino-type gambling, although many Japanese like to gamble. Government-sanctioned legal gambling is allowed on horse races, bicycle races, and motorboat races. Another form of legal gambling is the *pachinko,* or pinball machine. There are thousands of *pachinko* parlors all over Japan, where many people play for fun or for money and merchandise. Informal gambling is frequently done in mah-jongg parlors and on golf courses.

Although gambling itself may not be a major attraction for the average Japanese visitor, many of those who visit Las Vegas, Reno, Atlantic City, Macau, Walker Hill in Seoul, or the Gold Coast of Brisbane, Australia, enjoy gambling there.

Japanese men are rather notorious in many parts of the world for their "adventures with foreign women." They want to go to hostess bars and nightclubs to enjoy female companionship, as they do in Japan. At many popular foreign destinations there are hostess bars that employ local women to cater to Japanese male patrons almost exclusively. X-rated movies and pornographic videos or compact disks sold to Japanese visitors, and escort services advertised in Japanese undoubtedly stimulate this desire to experience sexual encounters. Reportedly, many Japanese men still go to Korea, Taiwan, Thailand, or the Philippines on a "sex tour," despite the fear of the AIDS epidemic. This type of tour has been severely criticized as immoral and shameful in the public media, but it is considered a necessary evil for a certain sector of the tourist industry. Historically, control of prostitution has always been a serious problem at many tourist destinations around the world.

Chapter 3

Visitor Profile and Market Segmentation

Effective marketing to Japanese travelers requires a good understanding of the travelers' profile and market segmentation because the travelers in each segment demand different accommodations, services, and tour activities. The most important segments are the honeymooners, young female office workers, student travelers, "full-mooners," senior citizens, middle-aged women, family group travelers, businessmen, rich business executives, and conventioneers. The Japanese travel market can be analyzed further based on the purpose of the trip, preferred destinations, travel companions, travel duration, and the amount of travel expenditure.

Profile of Japanese Travelers

Japanese travelers differ from European, American, or Australian travelers in their demographic characteristics and travel patterns. The majority of Japanese visitors are much younger. Japanese people are more likely to travel overseas before taking on a responsible position in their career paths; young women are also more likely to go abroad before getting married.

According to a survey by the Japanese Ministry of Justice, the median age of Japanese travelers is between 20 and 29 years. Of the 11,923,620 travelers surveyed, 56.6 percent were males and 43.4 percent were females. Of the male travelers, 2 percent were under 9 years old, 4 percent were between 10 and 19, 17.2 percent were between 20 and 29, 21.3 percent were between 30 and 39, 24.3 percent were between 40 and 49, 16.3 percent were between

50 and 59, and 11.5 percent were 60 or older. Of the female travelers, 2.5 percent were under 9 years old, 6.9 percent were between 10 and 19, 39.9 percent were between 20 and 29, 14.6 percent were between 30 and 39, 12.8 percent were between 40 and 49, 13.0 percent were between 50 and 59, and 10.3 percent were 60 or older.[1]

The survey notes that 16.2 percent of female travelers were single women, and of those 2.2 percent were students, 10.9 percent were young workers, 4 percent were older workers, and 1.3 percent were nonworking. Of those who were married, 6.6 percent were honeymooners, 5.6 percent were homemakers working outside the home, and 3.7 percent were homemakers not working outside the home. Of the male travelers, 5 percent were single, and 14.6 percent were married. Further analysis shows that 18.2 percent of Japanese overseas travelers were men and women between 45 and 59, 8.5 percent were 60 and over, and 11.3 percent were "full-mooners."[2]

Market Segmentation

Honeymooners

Honeymoons are a Western custom recently adopted by Japanese society. Today it is very common for young Japanese couples to take a honeymoon trip overseas. Groups of Japanese honeymooners began visiting Hawaii in the early 1970s, when the Japanese government lifted restrictions on foreign exchange. In those days, it was considered romantic for Japanese newlyweds to spend five or six days of their honeymoon in Hawaii, the "Paradise of the Pacific." In fact, in the 1970s more than 40 percent of young Japanese visitors to Hawaii were honeymooners.[3] Today Hawaii is still the most popular honeymoon destination, although the number of honeymooners has decreased relative to other types of travelers. In the past several years, Australia has become another popular destination for more affluent Japanese honeymooners. Other popular honeymoon destinations are Guam, Saipan, Hong Kong, Singapore, France, England, Germany, Switzerland, Italy, Greece, and Spain.

The Japanese honeymoon market has continued to be the most lucrative market segment for both Japanese tour wholesalers and for the local tourist industry. Japanese honeymooners are the best customers for them because they stay at luxury hotels, eat in fine restaurants, take deluxe tours, and buy many expensive gifts.

The ideal marriage age for Japanese men is considered to be between twenty-six and twenty-eight, and for Japanese women, between twenty-three and twenty-five. Many Japanese couples still get together through *miai kekkon* (arranged marriage), although *ren'ai kekkon* (love marriage) is considered a more romantic way of finding a husband or wife. Friends of the couple's parents and other relatives often act as *nakoodo* (marriage go-betweens). There are also many professional *kekkon soodanjo* (matchmaking services) in Japan that successfully arrange marriages—for a handsome membership fee. The go-betweens and the matchmaking companies do their best to match each marriage candidate based on his or her age, level of education, occupation, social and economic status, hobbies and interests, and family background. Those who marry through arrangements tend to have a much shorter courtship period, perhaps six months or one year at most. Some observant Westerners half jokingly say, "Now I know why Japanese newlyweds do not kiss each other in public. They may even look awkward when they are holding hands and walking around." However, the real reason for such restraint is that in Japan public displays of love and passion are still considered unnatural and embarrassing, even between honeymooners.

The choice of a honeymoon destination is determined not only by the honeymooners' preference, but also by both of their families' financial ability and social status. Because the costs of the wedding ceremony, reception, and honeymoon trip are exorbitant in Japan, parents of both the bride and groom must help pay for much of these costs. In other words, honeymooners from affluent families go to Europe for a honeymoon; those from moderately well-off families may go to Australia or Hawaii; and those whose families have less tend to go to Singapore, Hong Kong, Guam, or Saipan. The honeymooners must also consider their families' social status in choosing a honeymoon destination because the wedding and the honeymoon are a display of the family's wealth and status in the eyes of their friends, relatives, and business associates. In fact, Japanese business executives and politicians often use their sons' wedding parties as "business-social events," where they establish or renew important interpersonal networks. At Japanese wedding parties, the guests are expected to bring *kekkon yuwai* (monetary gifts for the wedding) in a special envelope, which can be between $300 and $1,000, depending on their social status and the nature of their relationship with the host families. The amount of money received from every guest must be carefully recorded because at least the same amount should be returned in the future to the givers when one of their family members gets married. Ordinarily, most of the monetary gifts are used to defray the cost of the wedding reception and *hiki-demono* (return gift for wedding guests), and the rest of the money is used for the couple's honeymoon trip and for buying souvenirs.

Another factor determining a honeymoon destination is the availability of good honeymoon package tours. Japanese honeymooners actually buy package tours and travel in groups together. In fact, approximately 83 percent of Japanese honeymooners still use tour packages for their overseas trips.[4]

There is one other important cultural factor (or superstition) that influences the wedding day. It is the traditional custom to choose a good wedding day based on the annual calendar issued by Shinto shrines. The "lucky days," called *taian* and *tomobiki*, are reserved for happy events such as weddings, groundbreaking ceremonies, and the opening of new businesses. There are five *taian* and five *tomobiki* each month, and it is also considered desirable to depart on honeymoon trips on these days. Sunday and Monday departures are also considered the most convenient because most weddings in Japan are held on Sundays. The luckiest wedding days are *taian* and *tomobiki* that fall on Sundays. On these days wedding halls are fully booked, and international airports are full of honeymooners. Spring and autumn are considered the best wedding seasons, although June weddings (adopted from Western culture) are becoming popular among Westernized young Japanese. This fad of the June bride is being promoted actively by Japan's bridal industry and tour wholesalers. The well-publicized royal wedding of Crown Prince Akihito and Ms. Masako Owada, held on June 9, 1993, might make June weddings more fashionable in the future.

The length of honeymoon packages is a minimum of four days and a maximum of ten. For example, a honeymoon package tour to such nearby destinations as Guam, Saipan, Hong Kong, or

Singapore would be three nights and four days. Hawaiian honeymoon packages are usually between six and eight days. Honeymoon tour packages to a huge country like Australia are not much longer. A honeymoon tour itinerary, covering Sydney, Melbourne, Brisbane, and the Gold Coast, is only eight or nine days. By any Western standard, this type of honeymoon tour package would be too short. It would never provide ample leisure time for the honeymooners. However, this rushed itinerary reflects the Japanese travel habit of packing in lots of activities during a short period of time. Another reason is that most Japanese employers are not willing to grant a leave of absence for more than five working days. In other words, honeymooners are expected to plan an overseas trip lasting no more than one week with two weekends.

A popular variation on the honeymoon tour package is the combination of the wedding and honeymoon in one trip. Many Japanese couples are eager to have a more romantic Western-style wedding. Today, it is considered very fashionable to have a wedding ceremony at a famous Christian church in a foreign country, although most Japanese are not Christians. In fact, many Japanese ask for a Shinto blessing when they are born, a Christian wedding when they marry, and a Buddhist funeral when they die without any feelings of contradiction. For example, the "Romantic Wedding in Hawaii" has been popularized by the Hawaiian weddings of several Japanese singing idols and famous show business personalities. A typical combination package includes air transportation, transfers by limousines, rental of a wedding gown for the bride and formal wear for the groom, flowers, a church wedding ceremony fee, marriage certificate, photographs and/or videotapes, hotel accommodations, a wine and fruit basket, and a special dinner for two. The chauffeur is frequently asked to play the role of the bride's father, if her own father is not there for the ceremony. There are several Christian churches at popular honeymoon destinations that specialize in weddings for Japanese couples. These churches even hire bilingual ministers who can perform wedding ceremonies in both Japanese and English.

Young Female Office Workers

Female office workers, who are referred to as O.L. ("office ladies"), are the second largest group of Japanese travelers. "O.L."

implies that they are pretty, sophisticated, and well mannered. The majority of these women are single and live with their parents. If they are married, they generally do not have any children. They range in age from eighteen to thirty-five, but most of them are between twenty and twenty-five. Despite some changes in Japanese women's status brought about by new labor laws and feminist movements, the traditional social custom of Japan still demands that "good girls" get married around twenty-five years old. When they get married, they are under strong social pressures to stay home, bear children quickly, and become full-time homemakers who will devote all of their time to important family matters. Knowing that they will most likely be forced into this predicament, most single women want to travel to foreign countries and try to enjoy themselves before becoming totally tied down.

Until several years ago O.L.s were nicknamed *dokushin kizoku*, or "bachelor royalty," and were considered the richest segment of Japanese travelers, who "spent money like water." Despite the recent recession in Japan, they still travel frequently to overseas destinations and spend a lot of money. The difference, however, is that these office workers are no longer as carefree and extravagant in spending as they were once claimed to be. They are generally quite price-conscious and well informed now about tour costs, souvenir stores, merchandise, and visitor attractions. They are more likely to use minicalculators to convert every price tag into Japanese yen before buying anything. They collect many tour brochures, pamphlets, and read guidebooks before they decide on what they are going to do during their overseas trips.

The most popular destination for female office workers is the United States because their lives have long been influenced by American culture and mass media. These workers enjoy visiting Honolulu, San Francisco, Los Angeles, New York, Washington, D.C., Boston, New Orleans, Orlando, and other famous cities in the United States. In fact, of the 3.562 million Japanese visitors to the United States, 1.322 million were between twenty and twenty-nine years of age.[5] Several years ago Australian cities, particularly Cairns, the Gold Coast, Brisbane, Sydney, Melbourne, and Canberra became popular among young Japanese women. Hong Kong and Korea are popular for shopping, Guam and Saipan are popular for water sports and tennis. France, England, Switzerland,

and Italy are also popular, but these countries are visited by more affluent young women. Young Japanese women also enjoy traveling to a different destination on each trip, but they may return to favorite destinations later. Many of them may return to a favorite destination for their honeymoon.

The average annual income of young female office workers is around $20,000 to $30,000, but they actually have a much higher discretionary income than their male supervisors. Since young women usually live with their parents or relatives until marriage, they do not have any housing costs. If they work for a large corporation, they can live in a single women's dormitory at a nominal cost. In fact, these women could probably afford to spend one-third of their annual income on overseas trips, if they chose to do so. Because many Japanese women are not as career oriented as their male counterparts, they might use up available vacation time without necessarily feeling the culturally influenced sense of guilt. Some of today's young women with professional skills prefer to work on a project-by-project basis under a short-term employment contract, then take long vacations to foreign countries between jobs. With this high discretionary income, ample vacation time, and a strong desire to travel, young female travelers are considered the most important segment of the overseas travel market.

Many young female travelers tend to buy inexpensive package tours that may include only air transportation, hotel or condominium accommodations, and transfers. They are willing to stay at any hotel as long as it is safe and has basic amenities. They want to make their trips as long as possible and experience things that local people usually do. They want to eat at the restaurants frequented by the locals, shop at typical department stores and discount stores, and take public transportation on their own when they go sightseeing. They may buy one or two prestigious brand-name handbags or watches for themselves, but they are more likely to buy practical things that they can use in Japan upon their return. They often eat inexpensive foods such as hamburgers, pizzas, and spaghetti and generally do not splurge on expensive meals. But they might try one or two gourmet meals at a nice restaurant for the experience, especially if that particular restaurant is advertised in the tourism literature they have read. Lately, it has become somewhat fashionable for office workers to leave their jobs and go to the United States, Canada, Australia, or England to study English for six months or one year. They say that they want to escape from the monotonous and boring pace of life in Japan and look for new challenges and a "refreshing experience" in a foreign country. When they return to Japan later, they hope to find a better job with their newly acquired English-speaking skills and their knowledge of a foreign culture.

Students

There are both individual and group travel segments in the students' travel market. The individual travelers are junior college or university students. They work part-time, save money, and take overseas trips during long weekends and vacation periods. Japanese parents usually reward their children with an overseas trip for successful entrance into a good school, graduation from a university, or landing a job with a prestigious company. Other relatives and friends give monetary gifts such as *nyuugaku yuwai* (celebration for entrance into school), *sotsugyoo yuwai* (celebration of graduation), and *shuushoku yuwai* (celebration for getting a first job). These monetary gifts can then be used for overseas trips by the students if they wish.

There is an old Japanese saying, *Kawaii ko niwa tabi o sasero,* or "Let your beloved child take a trip." Many Japanese parents still believe that having the children travel alone will make them more self-reliant and independent. They also believe that in the age of globalization their children should acquire *kokusai sensu,* or a "sense of internationalism," through foreign travel when they are still young. Consequently, parents are willing to support their children's overseas trips by paying either the entire cost or a part of it. Many young students take advantage of this generosity and travel with their friends to foreign countries.

Prior to 1987 the Japanese Ministry of Education and school officials restricted overseas trips by young students out of concern for their safety. Since the restriction has been lifted, this is the fastest growing travel market segment. An increasing number of junior high schools and senior high schools sponsor annual school excursions to foreign countries. The excursions are expected to meet the educational purpose of studying the languages, cultures, and social customs of the foreign countries visited. The itinerary should include visits to famous national monuments, historic sites, museums, art academies, and places of academic interest, as well as sightseeing visits and other typical tour activities. Some schools have the students stay with host families so that they have the oppportunity to interact. In order to facilitate better student exchange programs, more and more Japanese schools enter into sister school relationships with comparable schools in the United States, Canada, England, Switzerland, and Australia.

In the late 1980s, the Japanese Ministry of Education and the Ministry of Justice started the Japan English Teachers Program. Its specific purpose is to teach English and foreign culture to young Japanese students in rural schools throughout Japan by hiring young native speakers of English. The young college graduates come mainly from the United States, England, Australia, and Canada and are assigned to junior high schools and high schools as Assistant English Teachers or Coordinators of International Relations on a one-year renewable contract. Recently, the Japanese government changed the program to include German, French, Korean, and Chinese and renamed the program Japan Language Teachers Program. The Japanese government actually started hiring a smaller number of young teachers from Germany and France in 1990 and from Korea and China in 1992. They also teach their own native language and culture, just as English teachers do. The title of Assistant English Teacher was subsequently changed to Assistant Language Teacher, thereby including other foreign language teachers. Currently, between 2,500 and 3,000 young people from these countries are working in Japan under this new program. In some respects, they are unofficial youth ambassadors of their countries. Their frequent face-to-face contacts with young Japanese students in the classrooms will promote a strong interest in foreign travel among the students. These teachers can also provide excellent interpersonal links between the Japanese teachers of the host schools and themselves. This is one example of the Japanese government's efforts to internationalize all the people of Japan and to make Japan more acceptable in the international community.

Traveling students are generally not very rich unless they are from wealthy families. Students usually take inexpensive package tours or buy discount air tickets and stretch their budget by eating fast foods and wearing blue jeans and T-shirts. They usually do not buy expensive brand-name items or souvenirs. Many of them enjoy water sports such as swimming, snorkeling, diving, surfing, and windsurfing. They also play tennis and participate in skateboarding, skiing, golf, and other sports. Some female students may try aerobics at a local gym, but they tend to do more shopping than male students. University student clubs tend to go to one destination and stay there for two or three weeks of training. For example, a university swimming team may hold a swimming clinic in Hawaii for three weeks. The best golf team from the Japan University Golf Association may stay in San Diego and participate in an international golf tournament and compete against other golf teams from California universities. Or a ski team may go to Colorado and have a two-week long training camp.

In addition, more than 100,000 Japanese students are currently studying in foreign colleges and universities. The largest number are in the United States, England, Australia, and Canada. They also go to China, France, Germany, and many other countries to study whatever subject they have decided on.

Seemingly, Japanese students of today are members of a privileged class who can spend their parents' money. From the marketing point of view, the students are also an excellent potential market in the future. They will undoubtedly continue to travel more regularly than their predecessors, who did not have the opportunity to see foreign countries when they were students.

Full-Mooners

A "full-mooner" is a new Japanese-English term that refers to couples in their late fifties who take vacations after raising their children. Typically, Japanese husbands dedicate themselves totally to work until they reach high managerial positions or retirement, and Japanese wives spend their time caring for their husbands and children. Japanese couples hardly have time to travel as couples until they reach their full-moon years. This full-moon travel was initially promoted by Japan Railway Systems for domestic travel. But in recent years, it has become a fad for more affluent couples to take overseas trips as full-mooners.

Full-mooners usually buy more deluxe package tours from

reputable tour wholesalers and go to destinations where they can find good service without encountering language difficulties. They rely more on Japanese-speaking tour conductors or local tour company representatives because they usually do not speak English. They go to China, Hong Kong, Korea, Taiwan, Singapore, and Thailand, among Asian countries. They also visit Hawaii, Guam, Saipan, New Zealand, and Australia in the Pacific region, and London, Paris, Geneva, Copenhagen, Rome, and other major cities in Europe.

Since most full-mooners are much wealthier than younger Japanese visitors, they prefer to stay at nice hotels, eat good meals, and buy expensive items for themselves and for their family. For the majority of Japanese men, this full-moon trip could be the first time in many years that they are traveling with their wives since their honeymoon. This full-moon trip is often called *tsumi horoboshi ryokoo,* or "repentance tour," because the husbands are trying to make amends for the neglect of their wives for the years they were "married" to their jobs.

Senior Citizens

By the year 2000 in Japan the number of those in the sixty-five and older age group is expected to reach 21 million. With this large increase of the senior citizen population, the growth of the so-called "silver market" will outstrip the other markets. Before Japan attained the status of economic giant, it was common for three generations of one family to live in the same house and share living expenses and family chores as well. But with this new economic affluence, the nuclear family has become a more desirable family structure among the younger generations of the Japanese population. This means that grandparents are actually relieved of the responsibility of caring for their grandchildren. Grandparents are now free to spend almost all of the leisure time on their own. Most senior citizens are moderately affluent because they have accumulated substantial savings, have a house or apartment cleared of mortgage payments, and are entitled to a company pension and/or government pension. Many have abandoned the old Japanese idea of leaving a large inheritance to the next generation because their children no longer look after them as they used to. In other words, senior citizens have lots of time and money to travel and enjoy their retirement years with spouses and friends. Some older couples travel with their adult children (usually daughters) because they feel more at ease traveling with close relatives. This silver market is about 8.5 percent of the entire market,[6] and it is expected to increase rapidly.

Packaged tours for this market feature leisurely itineraries, the most experienced tour escorts, good Japanese meals, deluxe hotel accommodations, and slow-paced sightseeing tours. Sometimes the tours have an attending physician from Japan traveling with the group. In all cases, the Japanese tour companies sponsoring these tours make prior arrangements with local clinics and hospitals at each destination for emergency care by Japanese-speaking physicians. These tours cost between $3,000 and $6,000, depending on the destination, the class of service, and the quality of accommodations being provided.

Older travelers may or may not spend much money on souvenirs because they no longer have many social obligations. They may buy a few things for their daughters and grandchildren, and they may buy some local products as mementos. They might also be interested in arts and crafts, visiting museums, and doing some charity work for the local community they are visiting.

Today many older and very rich Japanese individuals own condominiums at famous foreign resorts. Or they buy time-share packages, which include condominium usage and a golf course membership. They might spend a few months of the year at these condominiums when Japan is either unbearably cold and dry or hot and humid. These travelers tend to stay longer and spend more money at foreign destinations. Some elderly Japanese citizens even reside almost permanently in foreign countries for health reasons. In this respect, Japanese senior citizens have begun to resemble elderly American and European visitors.

Middle-Aged Women

This market segment is unique to Japan. It clearly reflects the unique social structure of the average Japanese family and the roles that Japanese wives are expected to play. Young married women in Japan still hold a subservient position in their family and take on all of the responsibilities of running the family. "Good" Japanese wives are pressured to give up their careers, even if they are well educated and have a promising future. In addition to taking care of their husbands (and in-laws), they must take full responsibility for raising their children and managing the family finances as well. One of their most important responsibilities is making sure that their children study hard and pass several difficult entrance examinations from kindergarten to college. Japanese mothers are often called *kyooiku mama* (education mother) because they always push their children to excel in schoolwork. In Japan, graduation from a high-ranking university is the only guarantee that their child will be placed on a promising career path with a prestigious company. Consequently, mothers have virtually no social life outside the family, while their husbands enjoy a full social life with coworkers and friends. Japanese husbands are sarcastically called "absentee fathers"[7] because they rarely stay home. If they are hardworking salaried employees, they leave home early in the morning for work and come home late at night after the children have gone to bed. On Saturdays, they play golf with their coworkers or clients. On Sundays, they sleep or watch television, if they happen to be at home. The husbands play almost no role in educating their children. It is considered a "social" crime in Japan for a mother to leave her children in the care of baby-sitters or nursery schools and then go on a pleasure trip. Young husbands and wives almost never go out together for vacation trips by themselves.

In general, by the time these women complete their "duties" as education mothers, they enter middle age—late forties or early fifties. At this time, many wives start working part-time and save money for extra expenditures. (In Japan, married women are given full income tax exemption if they earn less than $900 per month.) Because Japanese husbands in this age bracket are still preoccupied with their own career advancement, they have no time for vacationing with their wives. Since it is also socially acceptable for older married women to spend leisure time without their husbands, they travel to domestic or overseas tourist destinations with friends. In fact, Japanese women prefer to travel with other women because then they do not have to cater to their husbands' demands. They often complain that they cannot enjoy a relaxing vacation if they have to prepare green tea, Japanese snacks and light meals, and wash clothes for their husbands in the hotel or condominium. Many middle-aged women also take overseas vacations with their daughters prior to the daughters' impending marriage.

Once again, middle-aged women can find the time and money to travel overseas as they could before they got married twenty or twenty-five years ago. They enjoy shopping, sampling different foods and drinks, and taking in cultural experiences at foreign destinations. Favorite destinations include Hawaii, Hong Kong, Taiwan, Thailand, Singapore, Malaysia, Guam, Saipan, well-known European cities, Australia, and New Zealand. Many package tours for this market segment leave ample time for shopping, gourmet dining, and visits to opera productions, classical music concerts, native arts and crafts fairs, and national museums. Sometimes these tours include opportunities to participate in gourmet cooking, listen to lectures on beauty and health care, and engage in cultural exchanges. Older women tend to take more short trips to different destinations because they tend to worry about family duties at home. This market will continue to expand, but only if it continues to receive the special attention and quality service that meet the specific needs of these travelers.

Family Groups

Family travel is the newest and most promising market segment in the Japanese travel market. Larger disposable income, the high yen value *(endaka)*, and the leisure-oriented life-styles of young Japanese families will significantly contribute to the growth of this market in the near future. In recent years, the most common form of family recreation has been family excursions on weekends with "my car" (a private automobile) to domestic destinations.

Family recreation trips are also promoted by the Japanese government. The aim of these government initiatives is to provide a more wholesome and healthy life for Japanese citizens, particularly for those who live in congested cities, by building facilities for outdoor recreation at government expense. For example, the Ministry of Transport has established 47 family travel villages, and 80 youth travel villages in national parks for outdoor recreation. Likewise, the Ministry of Environmental Protection has established 41 national recreation and natural parks for citizens' leisure," and 80 national leisure hot springs throughout Japan.[8]

There are many other resort facilities owned and operated by the public sector. These public facilities make it easier for the average Japanese citizen to enjoy family-style travel at very reasonable cost.

Today more and more families have begun to take family vacations to foreign destinations, as they find these trips more attractive and fashionable. Young Japanese parents who have already traveled to foreign countries while they were single or on their honeymoons will naturally want to take their children on overseas vacations. Unlike their parents, who endured poverty and hardship after World War II, the younger Japanese generation was brought up during the prolonged economic boom years of the 1970s and 1980s. Consequently, they are much more leisure oriented and do not hesitate to spend money on pleasure trips.

Most Japanese families travel when their children are still young (three to twelve years old)—before the children begin to study hard for high school entrance examinations. Because high school education is not compulsory in Japan, all junior high school students must take a high school entrance examination if they wish to enroll in the high school of their choice. And most of them must attend *juken juku* (cram schools) after regular school hours and on weekends. They have no time to take leisurely overseas vacations with their families. This period of hardship lasts several years, and every family member sacrifices leisure to help other family members who are *jukensei* (students preparing for entrance examinations). High school students in Japan must repeat the same process when they prepare for college entrance examinations. Most families will not travel again until the children enter a good university.

Since most traveling families have active young children, they prefer to engage in outdoor sports such as swimming, boating, camping, and visiting zoos and amusement parks. They prefer to stay in hotel rooms with kitchenettes or in condominiums, where the mothers can cook simple meals and snacks for the children. Families usually rent cars and drive around on their own. They shop in overseas destinations, but they tend to buy only those practical items that they can use for themselves. They usually take overseas trips on long weekends or during the summer vacation, winter break, or spring vacation. They generally do not stay more than one week or ten days, simply because working fathers in Japan cannot take a month-long vacation. Favorite family destinations include Hawaii, California (Disneyland and Yosemite National Park), Orlando (Disney World), Guam, Cairns, and the Gold Coast of Australia, where they can find sunshine, blue ocean, white sand, beautiful scenery, and ample children's entertainment.

Businessmen

Businessmen are another important travel market segment because Japanese companies still sponsor company-financed trips to many overseas destinations for a number of practical reasons. The most popular company-sponsored trip is the recreational trip for both management staff and employees. This trip to an overseas destination is not a genuine pleasure trip; it is a group travel to promote goodwill and friendship through informal contact and communication among the participants. It may even include a field trip and a short study session in addition to the usual sightseeing and recreational activities. For example, a Japanese discount store chain's "Hawaii recreation tour" includes visits to 7-11 stores, K-Mart, Costco, and Sam's Club and a one-hour lecture by an American professor on convenience stores in the United States. The tour members even have discussion sessions in their hotel rooms after their sightseeing tours.

Every member of the recreational tour group is encouraged to socialize with one another and to become acquainted with as many fellow workers as possible during the tour. Young office clerks, who would never expect to see the company president at work, may have the opportunity to talk with the president personally in an informal social setting. At the company dinner party, the president and other executives create many opportunities to chat with lower-ranking managers and employees. All of the participants, including top executives, may have a chance to show off their *karaoke* singing talent. In Japan, this intensive socializing during a recreational trip is considered the most effective means of building employee morale and engendering company loyalty. Disgruntled employees can voice grievances and personal frustrations to top management under the pretense of being intoxicated. This apparently impolite behavior by the "drunk" employees is usually excused by the targeted managers because they are expected to have sympathetic ears and open minds. Under certain circumstances Japanese managers even encourage their employees to vent their frustrations in order to prevent serious personnel problems from arising.

This travel market segment is expected to grow due to the new tax incentive provided by the Japanese government's initiative to promote more overseas travel among its citizens. As of 1987 the expenses for company-sponsored overseas trips have become tax deductible as employee welfare expenses, as is the case for domestic trips.

Incentive tours are another very common type of business travel. They are usually all-expense paid deluxe tours for business clients. Since Japanese businessmen conduct most of their business face-to-face, the incentive tours are invaluable in helping them to know their clients personally. Each year Japanese wholesalers and manufacturers invite the owners and managers of their client companies on trips to show appreciation for past patronage and to solicit future business. The sponsoring companies must ensure that their guests are treated well wherever they visit. Therefore, companies are willing to pay for deluxe hotel accommodations, fine dining, exclusive sightseeing tours, expensive golf games, and lavish dinner parties. The major purpose of these incentive tours is to give the top executives and key managers of the sponsoring companies the opportunity to meet and get acquainted with important decision makers of the client companies through days of intensive socializing. During dinner parties, the sponsoring companies usually hold a formal ceremony to give public recognition to those retailers and distributors who have attained the sales quotas in recent sales campaigns. These incentive tours are, in some respects, very much like sales convention trips sponsored by American life insurance companies to support and encourage their sales teams or individual agents.

Participants in incentive tours have ample funds to spend on souvenirs and optional tours because their travel expenses are paid for by the sponsoring companies. This incentive market will grow in the future because many Japanese companies will begin to sponsor incentive trips to exotic overseas tourist destinations. For the majority of Japanese travelers, domestic destinations are no longer exciting attractions. Tour wholesalers will need to find new and more appealing overseas destinations if they wish to promote this market segment.

Study tours *(kenshuu ryokoo)* to overseas destinations are popular among Japanese businessmen because these tours are usually a combination of study and pleasure. In addition, most of the study tour expenses are tax deductible and provide a legitimate excuse for otherwise busy executives to take a week or ten days off for an overseas vacation. Japanese businessmen are still seriously interested in learning from foreign countries, especially from the United States. Such organizations as chambers of commerce, associations of retailers, supermarket owners, fast foods stores, and discount stores frequently sponsor overseas study tours for their members. Many Japanese businesses send a few of their top managers or key staff members on study tours in the hope that they will pick up new ideas and useful information.

A typical study tour is escorted by a Japanese business consultant and an interpreter/tour conductor. The participants attend seminars or join field trips, but they also may play golf and enjoy parties. The Japan External Trade Organization, a semigovernmental trade organization, has always maintained liaison offices in key industrialized countries and has provided various kinds of assistance to Japanese study tours. Japanese chambers of commerce or trade associations organized by local Japanese businesses in major foreign cities also help visiting Japanese businessmen by providing proper introductions, up-to-date economic data, and information.

The participants' expenses are paid for by their companies, but they must submit a written report on their study tour. In most instances, they may be required to submit to the Japanese tax office written proof of business-related activities and expenses. They will buy souvenirs for their superiors, subordinates, and some clients, as they are obligated to do so. These study tours not only give them insights into business practices in foreign countries, but also provide many opportunities to cultivate friendship and goodwill among the participants. Serious leaders of study tours often insist on holding a *hansei kai,* or "review meeting," and have the participants discuss what they have learned from the field trip.

Wealthy Business Executives

There are two types of wealthy Japanese executive market segments: top executives of large corporations and owners of medium and small business enterprises. The top executives of large Japanese corporations may not receive monetary remuneration comparable to that of their American counterparts, but they are well treated while they hold top positions. They will be given overseas trips from time to time, with a young subordinate accompanying them to attend to their personal needs. In some cases, their spouses and children will be included as well. These executives are called *shayoozoku,* or "people with a large company expense account." They are authorized to spend a large amount of company funds for entertaining important clients, friends, and family members. They are particularly good customers for airlines, hotels, restaurants, nightclubs, hostess bars, and souvenir shops. They fly first class, stay at deluxe hotels, enjoy fine dining, ride chauffeur-driven limousines, and play golf almost every day. Some companies give a pre-retirement trip to a foreign destination to those executives who have dedicated thirty, thirty-five, or forty years to their organizations.

Another market segment is the owners of medium and small business enterprises who are independently wealthy. They may be thrifty, but they have a lot of disposable income to spend freely. Today, many of these affluent businessmen travel overseas with friends and family members. They usually travel during the New Year's holiday, on long weekends, and during summer vacation. More affluent Japanese businessmen who operate their own businesses purchase resort condominiums and golf memberships at well-known overseas destinations. They often combine business and pleasure and go to different destinations ostensibly on business trips. They tend to spend a lot of money on hotel accommodations, fine dining, and golf games but may be more careful in spending because their money was earned through hard work and dedication. Japanese executives of both segments demand prompt and courteous service even in foreign countries because they are accustomed to being pampered in Japan. They seem to believe that money talks wherever they go.

Conventioneers

With the increasing popularity of overseas trips, attending international conventions at well-known tourist destinations has become commonplace among Japanese businessmen, physicians, scientists, and academics. In the past, Japanese conventioneers attended international conferences only as participants. In recent years, however, Japanese professional organizations have begun to sponsor their own conventions at well-known international resort cities. Japanese participants may even fly in chartered jumbo jets. They will either organize their own conferences or stage joint conferences with clubs or associations in the host country.

International conventions require additional services such as display setup, the hiring of competent bilingual interpreters, arrangement of pre- and post-convention tours, ground transportation service, and entertainment and social events as well.

Japanese conventioneers are good customers because they are usually affluent businessmen and professionals who can afford to participate in overseas conferences without financial difficulties. They stay at deluxe hotels, have dinner parties, enjoy golf games, and buy expensive sportswear and souvenirs. International convention business from Japan should increase if more foreign cities can provide good convention facilities and the personalized services necessary for successful conventions.

Chapter 4

Promotion Media and Other Promotion Strategies

The tremendous increase of Japanese travelers to many overseas destinations can be attributed to the extremely successful promotion of overseas travel via the various advertising media readily available in Japan. Television, radio, newspapers, guidebooks, magazines, posters, and billboards are effectively used to appeal to potential Japanese travelers. Since Japan is a very small island country with a large population and only one time zone, it is quite easy for all mass media to reach the entire population of Japan. Indeed, instantaneous communication to every corner of the Japanese island chain is easily attained if an advertiser decides to use national television networks, national radio networks, and national newspapers. Other promotion strategies for overseas tours are package tour catalogs, travel fairs, special events, and familiarization trips. All of these have been effectively used to facilitate the continuing expansion of overseas travel among Japanese people. The choice of media should be made based on the nature of the business, the market segment targeted, the type of tourist destination, and the amount of expenditure available for advertising and promotion.

Television

Japanese television media are one of the most efficient means of promoting overseas tourist destinations around the world. On the average, Japanese people watch television 3 hours on a given weekday, 3.21 hours on Saturday, and 3.44 hours on Sunday.[1] Japan has Nippon Hoso Kyokai (NHK), the world's largest public broadcasting system, with two major television networks consisting of 3,500 VHF and UHF stations throughout the country. Japan also has NHK Satellite TV 1 and Satellite TV 2. In addition, there are five major commercial television networks, Nippon TV (NTV), Tokyo Broadcasting System (TBS), Fuji TV (CX), Asahi TV (ANB), and TV Tokyo (TX), with 48 VHF and 55 UHF stations. Today, these networks are supplemented by other cable television stations and satellite television channels: Asahi News Star, CNN (Cable News Network), MTV (Music Television), Star Channel, Let's Try, Garoa, Space Shower, Sports Eye, Satellite Theater, TVK TV, Chiba TV, WOWOW, and Nippon Eisei Hoso. Major commercial television networks are also able to broadcast programs through their affiliate stations in all cities, towns, and villages throughout Japan.

NHK has the most financial resources, since it is the public corporation authorized to collect subscription fees from every household with a television set. NHK has two television networks: Sogo Terebi, or General Television, and Kyoiku Terebi, or Educational Television. Both networks provide regular travel or cultural programs on various foreign cities around the world. The NHK's first network provides both domestic and international news, sports, and entertainment programs similar to those of commercial television networks and the second network provides a wide variety of educational programs from foreign language lessons to courses on world geography, history, culture, politics, and international cuisine. Since the NHK networks can spend large amounts of money on programming without any regard to commercial success, the programs are usually far superior in quality, and consequently, they have tremendous mass appeal. Many of NHK's travelogues are filmed on location at well-known cities, tourist destinations, or historic sites in foreign countries. Some examples are *Umi no Shiruku Roodo* (Silk road of the sea), *Meien San'po* (Walking through famous gardens), and *Sekai no Matsuri* (Festivals of the world). NHK has added a new documentary series titled *Asian Highway*, which introduces various Asian countries.

Commercial television stations in Japan are fiercely competitive. These stations regularly broadcast programs featuring unique overseas travel destinations in order to draw the attention of viewers. The commercial television programs usually play up on exotic, romantic, or sexy themes meant to appeal to the sensual desires of the viewers. For example, travel programs on Hawaii, the Caribbean, the South Pacific Islands, or the Great Barrier Reef of Australia typically feature shapely bikini-clad young women with handsome, muscular men basking in the sun on white sand beaches, against the backdrop of the brilliant blue ocean, tropical flowers, and coconut trees.

Many programs feature outdoor sports such as golfing, tennis, snorkeling, scuba diving, yachting, deep sea fishing, jet skiing, surfing, and windsurfing. These programs are extremely popular among young Japanese sports enthusiasts wishing to go overseas to enjoy these activities. For the majority of Japanese people, these activities are neither easily accessible nor affordable at home. Other programs include cultural tours to historical sites in Europe, the Middle East, and Asia, as well as visits to famous gourmet restaurants and wine cellars around the world. Some of the more popular programs on commercial television stations are the Hawaiian Open Golf Tournament, Augusta International Golf Classic, *Tokimeki Marin* (Fantastic marine), *Subarashii Sekai* (Wonderful world), *Sekai Marugoto Hau Matchi* (World travel how much), *Shinsekai Kikoo* (New world travels), *Sekai no Shamado kara* (Through train windows of the world), and *Chikyuu Oishisoo* (Gourmet foods around the world).[2] Recently, the Tokyo Broadcasting System began its new programs, *Sekai no Kekkon Shiki* (Wedding ceremony of the world), *Sekai no Ie* (Houses of the world), and *Sekai Fushigi Hakken* (Finding mysteries of the world). In addition, most of the television commercials shown in Japan have been made on location at famous overseas resorts. Even short commercial messages can have a strong impact on the viewing audience and raise their curiosity and interest in foreign travel.

American and European movies are extremely popular in Japan. Most of the highly acclaimed Hollywood movies, both old and new, are shown as feature programs by many of the Japanese commercial television networks. Since all foreign movies are either dubbed in Japanese or have Japanese subtitles, the Japanese viewers have no problem understanding them. In fact, many programs are broadcast in a bilingual format *(tajuu hosoo)* so that Japanese viewers can listen to either the Japanese translation or the original foreign language when they view foreign movies.

Major Japanese tour wholesalers frequently use television commercials to announce the introduction of new tour packages, but they cannot use commercials to advertise details of individual tour packages. Television advertising fees are prohibitively expensive.

Radio

In Japan, radio is another effective electronic media for advertising overseas travel. NHK has two AM networks with 331 stations and one FM network with 506 stations. There are 11 commercial AM and 29 FM stations. The major commercial radio stations in the Tokyo area are TBS Radio, Bunka Hoso, Nippon Hoso, Radio Nippon, Radio Short Wave, Far East Network (owned and operated by the U.S. military), Tokyo FM, FM Yokohama, and Bay FM.

Despite the ever increasing popularity of television viewing, radio stations have been successful in maintaining a unique niche among the advertising media. This is due to Japanese people's habit of using the radio in several different situations. Young people almost always use portable radios to listen to music as they walk or ride taxis and trains. Most drivers turn on the car radio while driving their cars or trucks. Many small family-owned factories and retail shops allow their workers to listen to the radio while working. Fishermen, picnickers, and hikers all listen to the radio while engaging in their respective activities. Talk shows on overseas travel and various music programs are extremely popular among young Japanese listeners. Recently, American-style radio talk shows and music programs by English-Japanese bilingual disk jockeys have become very popular among young listeners. Michael Jackson, Janet Jackson, Madonna, Prince, Garth Brooks, Ray Charles, Elvis Presley, and other American superstars have become the idols of many Japanese. Music fans flock to American music stores to buy compact disks or cassette tapes of these singers when they visit the United States. Some of them even travel to U.S. cities for the purpose of attending concerts given by one of these idols. And recently, rap music has become popular among Japanese teenagers. They seem to enjoy imitating African American rappers in the Japanese language.

Cinema Advertising

"Cine ad" is a shortened form of the English words "cinema advertising." A very brief message shown just prior to a movie showing is considered an effective marketing tool for honeymoon destinations. Studies show that young single women watch more movies than young men and that brides usually make decisions on the honeymoon destination. Foreign movies can be especially effective for this purpose because they are shown as a "road show" (feature movie) with good publicity in major cities all over Japan. Undoubtedly, these movies introduce the viewers to the scenic beauty, exciting city or country life, beautiful shops, and fine restaurants of the foreign countries where filming took place. Movie video rentals are also extremely popular among teenagers and young adults.

Newspapers

Newspapers are the most frequently used media for advertising overseas tours in Japan, as the Japanese are still print-media oriented. The average Japanese household subscribes to at least two newspapers—morning and afternoon. Most Japanese businessmen subscribe to one or two regular dailies, an economic newspaper, a trade newspaper, and a sports newspaper. Japanese salaried workers (commonly called "salarymen") on the average, spend between two and three hours daily commuting to and from work by train, bus, and/or subway. They have ample time to read newspapers during this time. There are three major national newspapers: *Yomiuri, Asahi,* and *Mainichi;* two major economic newspapers; *Nippon Keizai* and *Sankei;* and more than eighty local newspapers, twenty-eight sports newspapers, ten major trade newspapers, and four English language newspapers. The total daily circulation is estimated to be approximately 50,000,000 copies. When these major national and local papers carry advertisements on overseas travel, they can effectively reach a large number of potential travelers. Since newspaper advertisements carry rather detailed information, the readers can find out the prices, itineraries, and terms and conditions of the specific tours in which they are interested. Special sales campaigns on inexpensive overseas tours are often promoted by using *chirashi* (advertising inserts). Many travel advertisements usually appear in evening papers, since it is assumed that the readers are more inclined to check the papers more carefully during after-work hours or at home around dinner time.

Smaller regional newspapers can also be effective, if they are used to provide special feature articles targeted at readers not usually exposed to extensive information on foreign travel. For example, Japan Airlines reintroduced Hawaiian vacations by inviting news reporters from twenty-five small regional newspapers from Okinawa to Hokkaido. Each reporter spent several days visiting Hawaii and reported on unique visitor attractions on four different islands. This series of small articles giving their eye-witness accounts made this campaign extremely successful.

In addition, there are many weekly or monthly tourist newspapers published and distributed free of charge to Japanese visitors at foreign destinations. These free publications have been effective advertising media for a large number of merchandise, tour products, and services. Visitors can find many pages of advertising and useful information in these newspapers.

Guidebooks and Magazines

Japanese people are avid readers, and travel guidebooks are the fifth most effective means to promote overseas travel.[3] There are hundreds of travel guidebooks on the foreign cities, towns, and villages popular with Japanese travelers. All major Japanese tour wholesalers have their own travel guidebooks and magazines. In addition to travel information, their publications include many advertisements from tourist establishments with whom they do regular business.

Prospective Japanese travelers, particularly young female office workers, generally buy several guidebooks and study them as they plan their trips. In fact, some of these travelers have more accurate knowledge and information about certain tourist destinations than the comparatively ill-informed local tour guides.

Magazines also provide effective advertising. Many magazines specializing in foreign travel have enticing color photographs of young people on beautiful beaches, golf courses, tennis courts, and ski resorts. Women's magazines advertise shopping, gourmet foods, Christian church weddings, and romantic honeymoons in famous overseas tourist destinations. Men's magazines emphasize golfing, surfing, deep sea fishing, scuba diving, hunting, and other sports activities. These publications provide ample travel information on almost every major tourist destination. There are detailed maps, information on souvenir shops, hotels, restaurants, optional tours, tourist attractions, sports, and recreational facilities. Most of these magazines also include a few pages of English conversation lessons and cultural notes for the readers' convenience. These pages provide essential English words, phrases, and sentences together with Japanese phonetic syllables *(katakana)* and translation, as well as tips on local customs and dos and don'ts for the various social situations they may encounter in foreign countries. The most popular travel/leisure magazines are *Chikyuu no Arukikata* (How to walk around the globe), Ab-Road, *Tabi* (Travel), *Rurubu,* Blue Guide, Hawaii no Magazine, *Ryokoo Yomiuri,* (Travel Yomiuri), and *Tabi no Techo* (Notebook on travel).[4]

There are other smaller travel magazines published and distributed at overseas tourist destinations free of charge. These magazines can be picked up by visitors from tour desks or magazine racks in hotel lobbies, shopping centers, and airport concourses. The magazines typically include a calendar of local events, shopping guides, tour activities, golf guides, entertainment guides, real estate guides, and long-distance telephone information. Since they are published either monthly or quarterly, the information is more up-to-date than that found in guidebooks published in Japan months earlier. These magazines are sometimes brought back to Japan as mementos and are passed on to friends and relatives who may be planning to visit the same destination later.

The most widely circulated travel magazines in Hawaii are *Aloha Street Express* by Travel Plaza, Inc., and *Guide To Hawaii* by Stone Publishing. Both magazines contain a variety of information and advertisements with color photographs of specialty shops, restaurants, products, and visitor attractions. They also have feature stories on Hawaiian history, legends, and local events of interest to Japanese readers.

Almost all international airlines have in-flight magazines written in both English and Japanese. These magazines are very useful in informing Japanese passengers about other destinations they may visit. The airlines can also inform passengers about other tourist destinations within a country that they have not yet visited.

Posters and Billboards

Other effective advertising media are colorful posters and bill-boards. In major metropolitan areas of Japan, there are many train stations, subway stations, and bus terminals where hundreds of thousands of commuters pass by daily. The huge corridors and walkways of multilevel mass transit stations are excellent places for putting up eye-catching posters on tourist destinations. A large number of smaller posters are placed in trains, buses, and subway cars to attract the attention of potential travelers among commuters. Large billboards and neon signs are also effective if they are displayed on high-rise office buildings or on the busy streets of big cities.

Package Tour Catalogs

Japanese tour wholesalers and travel agencies conduct vigorous and innovative sales campaigns with the effective distribution of package tour catalogs to the traveling public. They offer a large variety of package tours to popular tourist destinations around the world. And their attractive color brochures have many pages of photographs of major tourist spots, the ocean, white sand beaches, hotels, restaurants, and souvenir shops. They also contain departure dates, tour package prices, itineraries, and terms and conditions.

Because these tour brochures are readily available through very extensive networks of retail travel agencies in every Japanese city, prospective travelers can collect a few of these brochures, make comparisons, and decide on which tours to take. They are the most effective medium of promoting any tourist destination, especially if a major tour wholesaler decides to promote that particular destination.[5] Major tour wholesalers such as Japan Travel Bureau (JTB), Kinki Nippon Tourist (KNT), Nippon Travel Agency (NTA), Jalpak, Tokyu Tourist Corporation and Hankyu Express International, JETOUR, and other wholesalers fiercely compete with one another by distributing large numbers of color brochures through their own retail travel agencies. They are also the most important trendsetters for overseas travel for the Japanese. In fact, 38.8 percent of package tour users surveyed mentioned that they became aware of the package tours through the tour wholesalers' brochures.[6]

Direct Mail

Direct mailing of tour brochures to former clients and other prospective travelers is another means of promoting overseas travel. Computerization of files on former client name lists makes it easy for tour wholesalers to mail out an announcement on new package tours. Many of these companies have been promoting "travel clubs" in order to capture repeaters. They offer to the repeaters a special discount or privilege as incentive to travel again with them. This direct-mail method is considered one of the most effective and efficient means of promoting low-cost tours to younger travelers, who tend to travel more frequently.

Special Events

Certain tour wholesalers, as co-sponsors, participate in semiannual bridal fairs, usually held in February or March, for June brides, and in July or August for November brides. They distribute colorful tour pamphlets at these bridal fairs to advertise overseas honeymoon trips to the women attending the fairs. They also provide information desks to answer questions from prospective clients. Some tour agencies distribute tour pamphlets at music concerts by popular foreign singing stars, at movie theaters where foreign movies are shown, and at amusement parks on long holiday weekends. More aggressive tour agencies even distribute tour pamphlets at major train stations where large numbers of young Japanese usually congregate on weekends.

Travel Fairs

From time to time national, state, or city tourist organizations sponsor travel fairs and special promotions in order to generate a large number of visitors from Japan. The United States, for example, held the Discover America Fair in Tokyo, Osaka, Sapporo, and Fukuoka under the sponsorship of the United States Travel Service, and in cooperation with major American airlines, hotels, restaurants, and ground transportation companies. This travel fair also introduced the scenic grandeur of famous U.S. national parks, ethnic cultures, and local products. The state of Hawaii, under the sponsorship of the Hawaii Visitors Bureau (HVB) and the Department of Business and Economic Development and Tourism, regularly sends a team of Hawaiian musicians and hula dancers to Japan to attract Japanese visitors to Hawaii. The musicians and dancers present spectacular Hawaiian hula shows at many tourist-generating cities. Free samples of Hawaiian pineapples, macadamia nuts, and orchids are given to all visitors at the fair. Videotapes featuring Hawaiian scenery and enjoyable outdoor activities are also shown at the fair. Japanese language travel information is made available at vendors' booths so that prospective Japanese travelers can obtain necessary pamphlets on various visitor attractions, shops, and products in Hawaii.

Travel fairs or displays themselves may not reach a very large number of individual Japanese travelers, but they can be seen by a much larger audience if they are picked up and broadcast by Japanese television media as newsworthy events.

Trade conventions sponsored by the Pacific Area Travel Association (PATA) and Japan Association of Travel Agencies (JATA) provide excellent opportunities for promotional activities. Top leaders from every sector of the travel industry attend these conventions. Not only do the conventions inform participants about new trends influencing international tourism through lectures and presentations, but they also provide opportunities for travel vendors to hold face-to-face meetings with other interested parties from Japan. Since Japanese businessmen value interpersonal trust, establishing personal contacts at these conventions is extremely important in doing business with them.

Familiarization Trips

Many tourist destinations sponsor familiarization trips for Japanese tour wholesalers, travel agents, and travel writers in order to introduce new visitor attractions. International and domestic airlines, hotels, restaurants, souvenir shops, and ground transportation companies jointly take care of those who are invited free of charge (sometimes at a nominal charge) in exchange for future business, good articles, or news reports. A well-planned familiarization trip can be the most effective way of convincing tour wholesalers to include a destination in their new tour packages.

PART II

CATERING TO

JAPANESE VISITORS

Japanese visitors spent a lot of money before the burst of Japan's "bubble" economy in 1990, but recently they have become more conservative and concerned with getting value for their money. Visitors expect to receive quality service for their money when they stay at hotels, eat at restaurants, or shop for souvenirs. Because the standard of service in Japan is extremely high, Japanese traveling overseas expect to be treated at least as well as they are at home. The majority of Japanese visitors do not speak English, and they also bring with them Japanese cultural habits and social customs. Most Japanese have always lived in a monolingual and monocultural society where the ability to speak English and work with people from different cultures was not very important. They rarely interacted with foreigners unless their work specifically required them to do so. Therefore, it is unwise to assume that the cliché, "When in Rome, do as the Romans do," applies to most Japanese visitors.

At the same time, the Japanese language is one of the most difficult languages. Not only is it very different from English in pronunciation, syntax, and grammar, but it also reflects the vertical nature of Japanese culture and has several levels of politeness. Some Japanese gestures and other nonverbal means of communication are also quite different. It goes without saying that Japanese visitors' expectations, preferences, and social customs should be carefully studied, along with the proper use of Japanese language in various face-to-face situations.

Chapter 5

Hotel Service for Japanese Visitors

A hotel should be a home away from home for all hotel guests. It must offer the guests not only comfortable rooms, but also excellent personalized service, good food, and a safe and pleasant environment. If it is a resort hotel, it should provide entertainment, recreation, and sports activities as well. If it is a business hotel, it should provide additional services to clients that will help them engage in business activities during their stay. Business machine rentals, secretarial services, translation services, and good message services are very important for business guests. Motels should provide services such as ample parking, quick food service, clean rooms, and some entertainment.

Although the physical facilities of almost all Western-style hotels are very similar, hotel service is different from hotel to hotel and from country to country. In Japan, the hotels that are allowed to accommodate foreign guests are called *kokusai kankoo hoteru,* or "international tourist hotels." These hotels must be licensed by both national and local government authorities. The buildings and other physical facilities, the food service, management, staffing, and services of these hotels must meet the strict standards imposed by the governmental authorities with jurisdiction over specific areas of hotel operation. Every international tourist hotel has a decal of official approval displayed on the wall behind the front desk. One of the most important requirements is that the hotel have at least one or more English-speaking staff on duty at all times. In fact, English-speaking ability is one of the most important job requirements for all hotel workers. Many hotel workers also speak French, Spanish, Chinese, Korean, or Russian. And all Japanese hotels provide superb hotel service for their international guests. Consequently, when Japanese hotel guests stay at hotels in foreign countries, they expect the same high standard of service and personal attention always available in Japan. The management and staff of Western hotels need to fully understand the expectations of Japanese guests if they wish to provide excellent hotel accommodations and services.

Front Desk Service

In Japan, hotel workers are trained to be extremely polite and patient with hotel guests. They know never to argue or show annoyance, even if guests are demanding or unreasonable. They are also trained to interact with foreign guests whose language and culture are different from their own. In general, Japanese hotels have many more people working in guest-contact areas, with several front desk clerks and two or more assistant managers in the lobby. The managers greet the guests and help them at the front desk. The bell captain and porters are alert and ready to assist the guests with their baggage and other chores, and they all speak fairly good English.

In contrast, hotel workers in the United States, Canada, Europe, Australia, New Zealand, and other Western countries are trained to work efficiently but are not necessarily capable of handling non-English-speaking guests. Many of these hotel workers struggle to communicate, mainly because of language difficulties and a lack of understanding of the needs and preferences of these guests. If Japanese guests are on escorted group tours, they may not have any language problems because the bilingual escort generally handles the check-in. But front desk clerks must communicate individually with those guests not traveling with a group. With the increase of FIT (Foreign Independent Traveler) guests, clerks should have at least the minimum level of competency in Japanese.

Not having enough Japanese-speaking front desk clerks creates several problems in guest relations. Japanese guests often complain that non-Japanese-speaking clerks look away to avoid eye contact. They "run away" to look for a Japanese-speaking coworker and keep guests waiting for a long time. If they must speak with the Japanese guests, they make the contact very brief in order to avoid being embarrassed by their inability to speak Japanese. They sometimes make the excuse that they speak only a little Japanese and speak broken Japanese in a laughing manner. If the clerks cannot speak proper Japanese, Japanese guests may feel that the front desk service is poor. Some hotels have tried to meet this need by assigning one Japanese-speaking clerk on each shift. Or they often ask the Japanese tour escort or the tour company employee to act as interpreter at the time of check-in. Other hotels have only one telephone operator on duty, who is asked to act as interpreter between the front desk clerks and Japanese guests. These stopgap measures are not acceptable solutions for eliminating language difficulties. Other hotels believe that when Japanese visitors are in English-speaking countries, they want to speak English and prefer to be greeted in English. In many simple interactions at check-in and check-out English can be used, if the front desk clerks speak slowly and clearly. But they should never speak to the guests too deliberately or in a condescending manner, as if they were English teachers speaking to young students.

Some Japanese hotel guests prefer different types of rooms. Japanese couples, including honeymoon couples, prefer rooms with two twin beds rather than one king-size bed. This may sound strange to Westerners, but Japanese couples do not necessarily sleep side by side on the same bed or futon at home. A husband and wife may sleep in a different room, especially if the wife is nursing. A large Japanese family may want to have a large hotel room with several beds and couches or two adjoining rooms because they want to do everything together. Generally speaking, Japanese guests do not require personal privacy as much as Westerners might. They usually do not express love and emotion even in front of other family members.

Assignment of rooms must be done carefully if a group of people with different social ranks check in. The higher a person's social rank, the better the room should be. If this is not done properly according to the hierarchical order, group members will exchange rooms without consulting the front desk. For example, the president of a company might be assigned a small single room on a lower floor because he is alone, and the vice president might be given a large twin room on a higher floor because he is with his wife. The president would be very unhappy if he finds out that a subordinate has a better room. At the same time, the vice president would be ill at ease and unable to relax and might even try to offer the better room to the president. In another situation, when a company recreation tour group with thirty people is assigned fifteen rooms aribitrarily, ten of the rooms may be switched around among them because of many complaints from the group members. This will cause problems for the front desk clerk, the telephone operators, and the cashier. Clearly, rooms should not be assigned simply based on the number of parties or the alphabetical order of the guest list. The relative social rank of each individual within the group should never be ignored. It is also important to remember that Japanese guests prefer rooms with bathtubs, as their custom is to soak the entire body in hot water even during summer and to take a quick shower before and after soaking. All Western-style baths in Japan have a detachable shower head attached to a hose, which is used to rinse off. In general, Japanese women prefer to use the shower head rather than a French-style bidet.

Most Japanese hotels do not have a separate concierge desk, but they provide more services at the front desk. A typical front desk provides a mail service for the guests' convenience. The front desk clerk weighs the mail, places the correct amount of postage, and mails it for the guests. Major hotels also house a forwarding agency where the guests can ship gift parcels anywhere in the world without leaving the hotel. The forwarding agency staff pack and label parcels at the guest's request. Some hotels offer facsimile transmission services, rental of word processors, video cameras and players, as well as baby-sitting services, and so on. Japanese hotel guests often complain that most Western hotels do not offer these extra services. One of the most frequent complaints is that guests must buy postage stamps from vending machines and mail letters themselves. They may not know how to use the vending machine or how many stamps to put on, but they cannot ask questions because they cannot speak English.

Being proficient in Japanese is critical to cashiers in order to provide good service to Japanese hotel guests, since misunderstandings involving money can cause serious trouble. The cashiers should be able to explain in Japanese the total charge and answer any questions regarding additional charges at the time of check-out. Most hotel charges are prepaid, but the additional charges for long-distance telephone calls, food and beverages from the room refrigerator, and meals charged to the room need to be collected. In some instances, local taxes and telephone service charges are seen erroneously by the hotel guests as unwarranted extra charges. The hotel guests may become irritated if they are compelled to pay charges without knowing what they are for. Most likely, the unhappy guests will complain to their travel agency after their return to Japan and have the agency verify the additional charges.

Another frequent complaint is that guests are not treated courteously at the cashier's window. When guests are in a rush to check out and need immediate attention, the cashier may take too much time to complete a simple transaction and the guests must stand in line for a long time. Even if cashiers are very busy, they should acknowledge that the guests are being inconvenienced and apologize for having them wait for their turn. And although this should not happen, the cashier may abruptly put out a sign saying, "This window is closed," and then leave without saying anything. Perhaps this cashier's shift has just ended or the lunch break has begun, but this type of behavior is a serious insult to Japanese hotel guests who have never experienced this treatment in Japan. To solve this problem, some hotels have begun to use a speedy check-out system that allows the guests to leave the hotel without stopping at the cashier's window. If guests decide to use this system, they must sign a consent form in advance, authorizing the hotel to charge all the expenses incurred to a credit card. The hotel in turn will send these guests a statement with detailed entries for verification a few days later.

Bell Desk and Baggage Handling

The bell desk is the central service center in the hotel lobby. The bell captain and the porters always come into direct contact with hotel guests almost twenty-four hours a day. They perform many chores for the guests: handling baggage, giving directions, providing messenger service, and arranging ground transportation. One serious problem unique to Japanese hotel guests is that they often leave their baggage unattended in the lobby. Because thefts are almost nonexistent in Japanese hotels, they tend to think that their baggage is safe once it is brought into the lobby. Porters must be alert and watch for outsiders who may come in and try to steal the baggage. It would undoubtedly help if the hotel management were to assign extra security guards or more porters to prevent baggage theft during peak check-in and check-out hours. Japanese guests are more likely to blame the hotel for the loss, even though the baggage might have been stolen because of their own carelessness.

Another problem is frequent misunderstandings about tipping. Even in Western-style hotels in Japan, porters do not expect to receive tips from hotel guests. This does not mean they are not allowed to receive tips, but management strictly forbids them to wait for tips. In fact, most American and European guests usually give tips anyway, so Japanese porters hesitatingly accept with a smile.

In order to avoid this unpleasant encounter between Japanese hotel guests and the porters, most tour packages include portage in the tour fare. In the case of group check-in or check-out, porters do not see the guests in their rooms at all. They bring the baggage while the guests are out for a tour orientation or shopping after check-in. The guests are usually asked to place their baggage inside their room door for early morning pickup at the time of check out. And all bags and suitcases are carried in a baggage truck to the airport. This advance inclusion of portage is an excellent idea for these reasons. In any case, diplomatic handling of the tipping problem is the key to smooth guest relations at the bell desk.

Special Services

The basic hotel operation system was originally imported from Europe and the United States, but Western-style hotels in Japan have upgraded their services to include a "Japanese touch." The hotels provide bilingual hotel directories and informational pamphlets, a closed-circuit television system, minibars, prompt room service, small safes, and good telephone, housekeeping, and medical services.

Bilingual Hotel Directory

A useful hotel directory for Japanese hotel guests should be in a bilingual format. It should include a welcome message from the general manager, a contract listing the terms and conditions of hotel accommodations; a map of the city and neighborhood; information on ground transportation; an illustrated restaurant guide with information on the types of food served, the floor and location, business hours, and proper attire; and information sheets with drawings explaining every service offered, including emergency and medical services, and telephone extensions for all services. (Hotels catering to visitors other than Japanese should have a multilingual hotel directory.) In many hotels, the hotel directory is also shown on closed-circuit television.

Closed-Circuit Television System and Newspapers

Today, satellite and cable transmission of electronic signals has made it possible to receive television programs from all over the world instantaneously. Japanese travelers can view news from Japan via satellite and enjoy local Japanese language television programs if their hotel subscribes to these channels. These television programs not only help them keep up with current news from Japan, but they also help reduce anxiety and homesickness. In Japan, English-speaking hotel guests can tune in to CNN news from the United States and other international news from London, Moscow, Beijing, South Korea, Hong Kong, Singapore, Sydney, and other major cities. Japanese viewers can see the same news programs either in Japanese or in the original language. Tourist hotels that cater to a large number of Japanese visitors should provide similar bilingual broadcasts and hotel information through their own in-house television system.

For business guests, it is important to provide Japanese language newspapers (and English newspapers, if they are bilingual) so they can keep up with the news from Japan and local sources. Large hotels in major cities in the United States and Europe subscribe to *Nippon Keizai Shimbun, Yomiuri Shimbun,* and *Asahi Shimbun,* which are published locally via facsimile transmission. Other hotels provide daily news briefs from Japan to all of the Japanese guests free of charge.

Minibar and Room Refrigerator

Japanese hotel guests make good use of the minibar and snacks stored in the room refrigerator. As they are accustomed to using them whenever they go to hot spring resort inns in Japan, they will do the same while traveling abroad. These are very convenient amenities for them when they find it too troublesome to go to a restaurant or store by themselves.

Socializing with friends and relatives on the same tour is another reason why Japanese guests find the minibar and snacks very useful. While staying at a resort hotel, guests almost always have late-night parties in one of the rooms. They may drink and socialize until midnight or the early morning hours. In Japanese inns, the guests can find the minibar filled with a variety of liquors in small bottles and *otsumami* (snacks) such as salted peanuts, cooked dried fish, dried octopus and squid, rice crackers, beef jerky, smoked salmon, and salami. If the hotels do not provide these things, they will go out and buy them from nearby stores. Some hotels in Japan have vending machines on certain floors where guests can buy snacks and cans or bottles of beer, whiskey, and sake. Many convenience stores in the hotel district capitalize on this particular Japanese habit and make money by selling almost everything they need for their private parties.

Prompt Room Service

Japanese hotel guests use room service more frequently than do American and European hotel guests. The Japanese generally have meals brought up to their rooms whenever they stay at Japanese inns. In almost all Japanese inns, dinners are served in the guests' room by a kimono-clad employee even today. (Breakfasts are served in a large dining room, although each table is assigned to the guests by room numbers. Lunch is not usually included in an overnight hotel package.) Western-style hotels in Japan do not provide the same personalized service as that found in Japanese inns, but the room service at these hotels is still excellent.

Many Japanese guests complain that room service in foreign hotels is very slow and that mistakes are often made in taking orders. They become disgruntled if they have to wait more than thirty minutes for a breakfast order, and then when the order is brought up to the room, the coffee or tea has become lukewarm. When room service clerks make mistakes, the guests might accept the wrong order without complaining directly, perhaps due to language difficulty, but they will undoubtedly complain to their travel agency afterward and will not return to the hotel again.

One way to overcome this communication problem is to print room service menus in both English and Japanese and to put corresponding numbers on each menu item. It would also be helpful to have color pictures of popular items in the menu. Ordering by number may help minimize mistakes, especially if the guest finds it difficult to place orders in English. Many Japanese hotels put a bilingual breakfast room service form in each room that lists two or three different choices of breakfast, from which the guest can make choices of juice, coffee, tea, eggs, meats, toast, muffins, rolls, and so on. The guests can simply make a check mark on the items they want and also indicate when they want the order delivered. This order form needs to be placed outside on the doorknob before midnight for pickup by the room service staff. This way, orders are delivered on time and without mistakes. This is an excellent service for those guests who need breakfast very early, before hotel restaurants are open.

Small Room Safe

Japanese visitors are easy targets for thieves and burglars because they are known to carry a lot of cash. They also tend to be very trusting, and they may leave valuables out in the open in their rooms. They may think that any hotel is a safe, private area reserved for hotel guests only, since that is the case in Japan. Sometimes they may intentionally leave their room door ajar to avoid getting up and answering the door when they are expecting their friends. (The group leader of a large party often makes this mistake.) Unlike resort hotels on the Pacific islands, Japanese hotels have fewer entrances and have plain-clothed security staff and managers keep a close eye on any strangers who may enter the hotel premises.

Hotel management should encourage each Japanese guest to use the small safe in the hotel room for money, passports, jewelry, and other valuable items. If guests have large amounts of cash, expensive jewelry, or other valuable personal possessions, they should be urged to use the hotel's main safe. It is also important for hotel security to warn Japanese guests never to open room doors to strangers in order to avoid possible dangers of burglary or even assault.

Good Telephone Service

Good telephone and message services are important to Japanese hotel guests because they generally want to keep in touch with their families and business associates. They may make several long-distance calls from their rooms even during a short stay. They may also need to call friends or family members in other rooms to discuss plans for sightseeing, shopping, or sports activities, as they rarely go their separate ways.

One of the most difficult tasks for hotel telephone operators is to identify and pronounce Japanese names correctly. If they are not familiar with the Japanese language, some Japanese names may be difficult to distinguish. Such family names as Ishihara, Ichihara, Itamura, Itoyama, Isayama, Nishihara, Nishihama, and Nishiyama may sound confusingly similar to them. At the same time, the names are not easy to remember. Another problem is differing romanized spellings of the same name. For example, "Inoue" may be spelled "Inouye," "Nakata" spelled "Nakada," "Ota" spelled "Ohta," and "Ueda" spelled "Uyeda." Japanese first names are even more difficult to remember due to many variations. Traditional first names for males end with o and for females with ko or yo. But modern names are harder to differentiate, because Hiromi, Kaoru, or Chiaki can be either a male or female name. Such long first names as Atsutaka, Hirofumi, Junshiro, and Masahiko are hard to pronounce. Still another problem is that many guests with the same last names, such as Tanaka, Sato, and Suzuki, could be staying at the same hotel. They may even have the same initials. In this case, operators should try to identify them by their tour group, place of residence, company affiliation, date of check-in, and number in the parties. One more possible problem is that the Japanese often state their last names first, and then their first names. If operators are not sure, they must ask whether the name is the last name or first name before they can proceed to help the callers. Hotel operators should become familiar with common Japanese names and learn to differentiate between them. At the same time, they should learn to pronounce Japanese names correctly. Mispronouncing a hotel guest's name is quite an insult, since every person, Japanese or not, cherishes his or her own name.

Wake-up calls are important for Japanese hotel guests on a tight schedule. They may be exhausted and suffering from jet lag. Although hotel rooms have alarm clocks, they may have difficulty setting the correct wake-up time by themselves. It is the responsibility of the hotel operator to ensure that these guests wake up and get ready on time for an early morning departure. In many instances, tour escorts may be forced to call each room to wake up all of the tour group members if they feel they cannot depend on the hotel operator. Efficient and accurate wake-up calls are an essential part of good hotel service. (In Japan, this is often called *mooningu kooru*, or "morning call.")

Message service is another important responsibility of the hotel operator. If possible, telephone messages should be written in Japanese. It would also be a good idea to use a bilingual message form and write the message out in English as well. (Most Japanese can read romanized names.) If a telephone message is not picked up or responded to within several hours, a porter should deliver the written message to the guest's room. This service is critical, especially if the message is urgent or if it is for a VIP guest.

Japanese hotel guests should be informed about how to use the telephone in their rooms. One small but important difference is that they dial "0" to place outgoing calls in Japan, whereas they dial "9" for the same purpose in the United States. Some repeat guests know how to make long distance calls, but others may need the operator's assistance. There are two types of calls, person-to-person *(shimei tsuuwa)* and station-to-station *(futsuu tsuuwa)*. There are also two ways to pay for the call, as a collect call *(sen'poo barai)* or as charged to the room *(oheya ni tsukeru)*. The collect call may be easier for non-Japanese-speaking operators because they can obtain assistance from a Japanese operator on the other end.

Finally, there are two difficulties that need attention. Most hotels in the United States do not give out the room numbers of guests for security reasons; only the guests themselves can tell callers their room number. Japanese hotel guests and other callers often find this practice very inconvenient. Hotels in Japan give out the guests' room numbers freely unless the guests specifically ask the hotels not to do so. Another difficulty is with the extra handling charge (an additional charge on top of the telephone charge itself whenever the guest uses the phone for outside calls) for all calls that is routinely put on the guests' hotel bill. In other words, guests must pay this extra charge every time they make collect calls to Japan. At some hotels, this charge is levied even when the call does not go through. If guests make several collect calls, they will have to pay a lot of money for this service. Hotel management must explain all of these charges in Japanese in order to avoid misunderstandings.

Efficient Housekeeping

Efficient and considerate housekeeping is essential in satisfying Japanese hotel guests. At times, the housekeeping staff must cope with special problems because many Japanese guests are unfamiliar with Western-style hotel facilities. One problem is that some Japanese guests may try to bathe Japanese style in a Western-style hotel bathroom. First they fill the tub with hot water. Then they lather and rinse themselves outside the tub and then climb in for a long soak. If the bathroom does not have a drainage hole in the floor outside the tub, the bathwater will seep through the ceiling of the room below. (All Western-style hotels in Japan install a drainage hole in each bathroom to avoid this problem.) Sometimes guests unknowingly put the shower curtain outside the tub and cause the same problem. In most instances, when these accidents occur, they hesitate to call the front desk for help right away. Instead, they may try to wipe up the water by themselves, using all the towels in the room. Perhaps they are too ashamed to ask for help. Even though these mishaps rarely occur these days, it would be a good idea to post a sign in Japanese explaining how to use a Western-style bathtub.

Another problem is that a small number of older Japanese guests may not know how to use a Western-style toilet. They may try to squat on the toilet seat instead of sitting on it. A few women may throw sanitary napkins or other feminine-hygiene products into the toilet bowl. Again, it would be wise to post a simple sign in Japanese advising guests on how to use the toilet properly.

Because most Japanese visitors use a futon in their homes, they may not know how to tidy up their beds before going out. They may leave the bedspread and pillows scattered about the bedroom. When they check out they may leave the room doors open. Some guests bring a lot of food and drink into their rooms, such as instant cup noodles, instant miso soup packages, green tea bags, dried fish, and pickled vegetables. Since hot water is used to make green tea and miso soup, the bathroom sink often becomes a temporary kitchen sink. Guests may leave a lot of garbage in the wastebasket. Male guests are known to smoke a lot. The housekeeping department should alaways place more ashtrays in smoking-designated rooms. At times, guests are blamed for making cigarette holes on the blanket or the bedspread. A sign prohibiting smoking in bed should be posted to warn guests not to do this.

Laundry service may not be very important to Japanese guests because they generally stay only for short periods of time. If they do need laundry service, they tend to want it done quickly. (In Japanese hotels, guests can request a four-hour service for laundry, dry cleaning, or ironing.) All laundry and dry cleaning forms should be printed in both English and Japanese to avoid miscommunication. Because misplaced or damaged laundry can harm a hotel's reputation, the housekeeping staff in charge of laundry should be careful when handling guests' clothing. It would be difficult to settle claims once guests have checked out and returned to Japan.

One other problem is that Japanese hotel guests may hang their laundry (swimwear and underwear) out on the balcony or veranda in plain view of other guests. This is part of the "cultural baggage" they bring with them when they travel overseas. The Japanese believe that laundry should be dried outdoors instead of indoors for sanitary and health reasons. This is why the balconies of even the plushest condominiums in Japan have laundry fluttering in the breeze. (Standard Japanese weather forecasts include information giving sunny periods of the day for this purpose.)

Maintenance of Guest Rooms

Japanese hotel guests may call for help from the maintenance department for several reasons: perhaps they cannot unlock the sliding door to the veranda, or the telephone does not work, or the air conditioning is too noisy or does not make the room cool enough, or they cannot open the room safe, or the television does not work. Perhaps they flooded the bathroom and are in need of help right away. Such requests require immediate attention. If maintenance staff are not immediately available, the guests should be informed as to how soon they can expect help. It is very discourteous to have guests wait too long without knowing when the problem will be solved.

Some hotels in the tropics have serious problems controlling cockroaches, ants, and lizards. Japanese hotel guests from urban areas generally have a strong dislike or even fear of these insects and reptiles. Maintenance staff should respond to any call regarding pest removal immediately, as guests do not see such creatures back home and are truly afraid of them.

Solving Guest-Relations Problems

Japanese guests come from a status-oriented society where the customer is considered king. They can become unreasonably demanding and even obnoxious when problems arise. They may show their anger openly or they may try to hide it in front of others. Some Japanese business executives or politicians may shout loudly and scold the hotel staff, but most Japanese guests will not complain openly even when they are mistreated. They may simply show annoyance nonverbally and walk away from the situation. But when these guests return to Japan, they will bitterly complain to the tour agency that made the hotel reservation for them. They may also tell their friends and relatives about the mistreatment and persuade them not to go to that hotel. In some instances, the alleged mistreatment itself may not be too serious, but the way it was handled by the hotel management and the staff could become a real problem later. Hotel managers and workers should use several culturally acceptable ways of handling guest-relations problems.

The Importance of the Apology in Japanese Culture

Japanese comedians often make a big joke about making an apology. They get laughs from the audience by saying, "The Japanese live in an 'I'm sorry' culture. They are always apologizing and bowing to one another for this and that." Indeed, *sumimasen* (I'm sorry) is the most frequently used expression in Japan! In many instances, an apology is used merely as a means of expressing sincere concern or regret. It should not always be interpreted as an admission of guilt or of legal responsibility. A timely and sincere apology by the highest ranking person can solve many problems with the Japanese. This person may be the general manager, the assistant general manager or the front desk manager—whoever is on duty. For example, a Japanese hotel guest slips on the wet marble floor at the hotel entrance and is injured. The immediate reaction of a Western hotel manager would be to call an ambulance and have the guest taken to the hospital. The manager would probably not apologize and would avoid making any statement that might make the hotel appear liable for the injury.

On the other hand, a Japanese hotel manager would apologize first and show personal concern. The manager may even ride the ambulance with the injured guest to the hospital, if he feels it is necessary. He will ask the general manager to send a bouquet of flowers to the guest's hospital room with a get-well card expressing the hotel's concern. If the injury is serious, the general manager would undoubtedly visit the guest at the hospital and express personal concern. Should there be any litigation against the hotel over this accident in the future, the presiding judge in a Japanese court will generally take the manager's *sei'i* (sincere attitude) into consideration. A timely expression of concern and sincere apology in words and action can effectively smooth over many difficulties with the Japanese. It is a good idea to have a set of standard form letters of apology in polite Japanese language for use in various situations. The general manager should send the most appropriate letter immediately upon consultation with the Japanese guest-relations director. If the general manager feels that a letter alone does not suffice, he should send a proper gift to the mistreated guest along with the letter of apology.

Overbooking and Nonavailability of Desired Rooms

Overbooking of rooms is one of the most serious problems. Huge numbers of Japanese travelers tend to go overseas during the same long weekends and holiday seasons. For example, more than half a million Japanese people travel to several major foreign destinations during "Golden Week" (April 27 through May 5), the New Year holidays (December 28 through January 5), and the summer season (late July through the end of August). This unique travel habit of the Japanese can cause serious problems for many hotels trying to accommodate a flood of visitors at once.

Hotel reservation clerks must be extremely careful not to overbook rooms during periods of heavy travel by the Japanese. Clerks should aggressively seek cooperation from tour wholesalers who book blocks of rooms, and they should communicate directly with travelers who have made their own reservations. And it is always wise for reservation clerks to contact important repeat customers directly to ensure their arrival. Clerks should never cancel or make new bookings until they have checked and rechecked the occupancy status of every room in the hotel.

Should an overbooking occur, reservation clerks should not blame or scold the guests for not paying the required deposit or for not reconfirming their reservations in time. Instead, they should be patient and sympathetic. And clerks should not shift the blame for the overbooking to the tour agency in Japan. Such impoliteness will not solve the problem; it will only aggravate the situation. It is always a good policy to find comparable or better rooms at nearby hotels for hotel guests who have been inconvenienced.

Front desk clerks often face irate hotel guests who have suddenly realized there are no rooms available. Even if the guests are obviously at fault, the clerks should refrain from saying anything accusatory or impolite. They should be diplomatic and courteous, as it could be possible that the guests' names were misspelled or that the first and last names were reversed at the time of reservation.

Nonavailability of desired rooms is another serious problem at hotels. When advertising deluxe package tours, many Japanese tour wholesalers promise to provide specific types of hotel rooms.

For example, Look JTB's Waikiki Diamond Package Tours specify the hotel, the floors, the type of room, and the views from the room. One package that uses the Sheraton Waikiki Hotel has a brochure saying, "20th floor or higher, a medium suite or a large suite, ocean front with Waikiki Beach view, and straight check-in (no waiting for a room upon arrival)." If this particular type of room were not available, hotel guests who bought this package could become very upset. In Hawaii, most visitors want hotel rooms with ocean views. Consequently, Japanese tour companies have devised different categories such as ocean front, ocean view, partial ocean view, mountain view, partial mountain and ocean view. Some of these descriptions are misleading: a so-called ocean-view room might be in a hotel situated one block away from the ocean, where the guests may have to step out onto the veranda to see the ocean. A partial ocean-view room may have a narrow view of the ocean between other tall hotel buildings. The classification of Waikiki hotels adds to the confusion because they are further categorized as "on-beach" or "off-beach" hotels.

Whatever the reasons for the confusion, these problem must also be handled diplomatically. One solution would be to offer unhappy guests a desired room as soon as it becomes available. Another solution could be to send a letter of apology from the general manager, complimentary dinner-show tickets, and a basket of tropical fruits. Japanese guests in general will not willingly accept a partial refund, which would be the difference between the ocean-view and the partial ocean-view rooms. A polite apology and kind actions rather than a reasoned discourse will usually win friendship and cooperation.

Thefts and Burglaries

Since Japan is a very safe country, many Japanese visitors may not be careful about their possessions and personal safety. A recent Japanese government report states that many Japanese citizens traveling overseas were subjected to such serious trouble as traffic accidents, thefts and burglaries, drownings, rapes, and murders. The report also states that large amounts of cash, travelers' checks, baggage, cameras, jewelry, and passports were stolen from those unsuspecting Japanese travelers.

Hotel management and security staff should take immediate

action and show sincere concern should a theft or break-in occur. Japanese hotel guests who are victimized while on the hotel premises expect hotel management to apologize immediately, even if the hotel is not at fault. Security guards should not simply call the police and then stand around waiting. If a guest is injured, a Japanese-speaking doctor should be called immediately. If none are available, the hotel should contact the tour agency representative (or the local Japanese consulate if necessary) and help the injured guest feel safe and comfortable.

Some Japanese men may bring prostitutes into their rooms. Perhaps they are curious or want to have an "adventure" with foreign women. Often the guests are robbed of money, cameras, passports, and watches while asleep. In some instances, they may even be assaulted by the prostitutes. To prevent this, the security guards should sternly warn guests not to bring prostitutes into the hotel. At the same time, they should keep an eye on the prostitutes who may solicit these "adventurous" guests. In certain resort towns in Japan, there are many "love hotels" or massage parlors where men can buy sex without difficulty. They may feel they can do the same at foreign destinations.

Errors in Computing Charges

Unintentional errors in room rental and other charges can cause serious problems in guest relations. Japanese hotel guests who cannot understand English may feel they have been overcharged. One special problem with Japanese hotel guests is that they often use vouchers issued by their travel agencies. All vouchers have limited values, and face values are not printed on them. Some vouchers cannot be used for certain services.

Another problem is missing remittances from Japan. There are at least two possible causes of this: remittance for advance deposits may not have reached the hotel's accounting department in time for the guests' check-in, or the remittance may have been credited to the wrong account. Should this occur, clerks should call the booking agency in Japan at the hotel's expense to clarify the situation. Making guests pay twice would undoubtedly alienate them regardless of whose fault it might have been.

If possible, all hotels that cater to Japanese guests should provide invoices, statements, and receipts in both English and Japanese. Many English abbreviations of hotel charges are unintelligible to Japanese guests and may cause misunderstandings.

Lost and Found

Losing personal effects and valuables on a vacation trip can be a miserable experience for anyone. On the other hand, recovering a lost possession can be an occasion of great joy, especially if it is a precious memento, money, or passport. Hotels catering to Japanese visitors must have an efficient method of handling lost and found items, since guests generally leave for other destinations or return to Japan within a short time span and thus cannot easily fly back and claim lost items. Porters and housekeepers should be instructed to report immediately any items left behind in hotel rooms. Those in charge of lost and found should contact the guests immediately through the local tour agency or airline being used by the guests. They should not wait for the guests to contact the hotel later. An identification and description of the item, as well as the location where the item was found, should be carefully recorded, numbered, and dated for future reference as soon as possible. Lost and found items should not be left unattended for long because the guests may call to inquire about them shortly after check-out.

   In some instances, housekeepers may be suspected of stealing from guests. Since Japanese visitors usually do not have any direct contact with non-Japanese hotel workers in Japan, they may sometimes feel that "strange" foreign housekeepers cannot be trusted. Consequently, they might blame them for the missing items. True or not, a hotel's image may be tarnished if the housekeepers are suspected. The housekeeping manager should instruct the housekeepers not to move the guests' possessions around in the room,as some Japanese hotel guests have a habit of leaving valuable personal possessions lying around.

Emergency Medical Care

Visitors who becomes ill or injured in a foreign country will naturally become very worried if they cannot obtain prompt medical attention. They may become agitated or even distraught, especially if they cannot understand the language spoken by the doctor and other medical staff. Many English medical terms are difficult to understand for those Japanese guests with limited English. Japanese visitors may be afraid to have non-Japanese-speaking doctors treat them because medical care is a very personal matter to them. Hotels catering to a large number of Japanese visitors should have their own medical clinic staffed with bilingual doctors and nurses. Establishing good working relationships with a few local hospitals will become more important than ever, since many Japanese people with chronic illnesses and disabilities are beginning to travel overseas. Some may have mild heart conditions, and others may need kidney dialysis treatments. More and more people in wheelchairs are also traveling.

At most major tourist destinations there are "doctor on call" types of medical services for Japanese-speaking patients. Travel insurance companies in Japan provide a list of Japanese-speaking physicians for their clients' convenience. Local tour companies also provide assistance to their clients who may suddenly become ill during vacation trips. Hotel management should also be aware of medical services available locally and instruct the front desk, telephone operators, and concierge desk to keep an up-to-date list of services on hand.

The care of a sick hotel guest requires extra attention and special service. First, if the guest does not speak English, a competent Japanese interpreter should be brought in to ask the guest what is wrong. Second, a person should be assigned to take the guest to the clinic without delay. In cases of serious illnesses or medical emergencies, the guest's family in Japan should be contacted immediately. In the meantime, the local tour company should be asked for assistance. (Most Japanese tour companies take on the responsibility of caring for sick clients, although they are not legally responsible.) Third, immediate action should be taken, with little concern as to who will pay for the medical care. Almost all Japanese visitors buy travel insurance and are generally quite responsible about paying medical bills. If it is a life or death situation, the manager-in-charge should work with a representative of the local Japanese consulate. Finally, hotels should keep on hand a copy of a Japanese-language booklet on medical care for quick reference.

Chapter 6

Food and Beverage Service for Japanese Visitors

Tabi wa mikaku (travel is to eat tasty food) is a frequently used catchphrase for travel advertising in Japan. Indeed, tasting famous local foods and drinking good local beverages are important visitor attractions. Japanese visitors will usually find great pleasure in tasting fish, shellfish, meat, vegetables, fruits, liquor, and other items in the village or town where they are harvested or produced. Every tourist destination heavily advertises all sorts of *meibutsu* (famous products) considered attractive to the visitors. Travel magazines, newspaper advertisements, guidebooks, and tour package pamphlets all include what to eat and drink and which restaurants to visit at every tourist destination. Most Japanese visitors try to have a few of the most famous foods and drinks wherever they visit.

In Japanese culture, eating and drinking are also extremely important social activities. Japanese people always find certain legitimate reasons to eat and drink when they get together. For them, eating and drinking are not only for gastronomical enjoyment, but also for promotion of friendship and business relationships. They invite each other to lunch or dinner when they meet for the first time, and they do the same when they need to meet again. When they go on a group tour, they usually have a welcome party and a *sayonara* party to socialize with each other. This social habit makes Japanese visitors very good restaurant customers.

Restaurant management should know what kinds of food and drink are preferred by Japanese visitors, and restaurant workers should know how to serve them to satisfy expectations. Japanese visitors may behave differently than Westerners because they bring with them Japanese manners and habits. Many are not familiar with Western-style restaurant services, and are often confused about Western manners. In many instances they will need extra care and special attention.

Popular Food and Beverages among Japanese Visitors

Many Japanese visitors are "curious gourmets" who want to taste all kinds of food and beverage whenever they travel to foreign countries. They also like to dine at a few of the most prestigious and famous restaurants at a particular tourist destination. Each of these restaurants must have house specials that customers can identify with the restaurant. Japanese visitors usually take a lot of photographs, and upon their return they will probably enjoy talking about the restaurants and the famous dishes and drinks they tried. They like to eat American, Chinese, Japanese, Italian, French, Thai, Vietnamese, and many other different ethnic cuisines. They also like to drink famous whiskeys, wines, and other locally brewed alcoholic beverages for new experiences. Authentic ethnic foods and beverages are very important for Japanese travelers.

American Food

A typical American dish considered popular among Japanese visitors is the steak and lobster combination plate. This dish is an excellent choice for many of them because both steak and lobster are very expensive in Japan. New York steak, sirloin, filet mignon, and prime rib are popular among younger Japanese visitors. Japanese customers often complain that American steaks are very big but too tough and not very tasty. They prefer a smaller steak of high quality to a jumbo steak of poor quality. Maine lobsters, Blue Point oysters, cherrystone clams, soft-shell crabs, Alaskan salmon, and various local fishes are also favorites of the Japanese. And in recent years American breakfasts have become popular, as Western-style hotels in Japan serve them in more or less the same way. American fast-food chains such as McDonald's, Burger King, KFC (formerly Kentucky Fried

Chicken), Taco Bell, Pizza Hut, Denny's, Mr. Donut, and Baskin-Robbins have also turned Japanese people into American-food lovers.

Live Maine lobster dishes are very popular among almost all Japanese visitors. Today Japan imports tons of live lobsters mainly from New Zealand, Australia, and the United States, but lobster dinners are still very expensive in Japan. A one-hundred dollar lobster dinner in the United States is considered a big bargain, because a similar dinner may cost between two hundred and three hundred dollars in Japan. Many Japanese customers prefer to have their lobster baked with mayonnaise and bread crumbs, but older Japanese prefer to have it steamed or boiled and to eat it with *sanbaizu* (soy sauce with vinegar and lemon juice) instead of melted butter. Others prefer to eat it raw, sashimi style, with *wasabi* (Japanese green mustard).

Buffet meals have a certain appeal to Japanese visitors. Since they can plainly see all the dishes on display, they do not need to look at a big English menu. A buffet-style service is also more convenient for the restaurant management because it can help solve any language problems and save a lot on labor costs. However, Japanese customers generally do not like buffet-style meals for every breakfast, lunch, and dinner if they must go through a buffet line that has the same foods every day of their stay. Some items on the buffet counter should be changed daily for variety. Many buffet-style restaurants at major Japanese visitor destinations now include miso soup, pickled vegetables, salted plums, steamed rice, and sushi to make their buffet meals more palatable to their customers. It would also be very helpful if the restaurant were to place small cards indicating what each of the main dishes are in both English and Japanese. The management should also realize that the buffet-style meal will not be appreciated by all Japanese customers. For example, some older Japanese men with high social status will feel embarrassed to stand in line and serve themselves. Spouses or young assistants may volunteer to help those who feel embarrassed and helpless.

Chinese Food

Chinese food has always been appreciated by the Japanese. Indeed, Japanese visitors often look for Chinese restaurants when they get tired of eating Western cuisine. They are particularly fond of seafood cooked Cantonese or Shanghai style. They like Dungeness crab, live shrimp, live lobster, oysters, and cherrystone clams. They also like Szechuan-style cooking. Sometimes, large parties of Japanese men will purchase a few bottles of Chinese wine and drink it hot in a small cup with rock sugar and lemon. One Japanese practice at Chinese dinners that differs from that of the Chinese is that they do not eat rice together with main dishes. In fact, they may not eat rice at all. If they do, they prefer to have it served with *zasai* pickles toward the end of the meal with Chinese tea.

Quasi-Chinese food, or "Japanized" Chinese food such as *ramen* (noodles in soy sauce soup), *gyooza* (pot stickers), and *chaahan* (fried rice) are extremely popular among young Japanese visitors on a tight budget. Several Japanese noodle restaurant chains have opened up hundreds of branch snack shops at major Japanese visitor destinations all over the world. Japanese visitors either eat such foods as meals or snacks, as they are inexpensive and taste the same as they do in Japan.

Japanese Food

The Japanese may seem to have become quite Westernized in their food habits, but the truth is that most Japanese people cannot stand more than a few days without having Japanese food. They even look for authentic Japanese food while traveling in foreign countries. This explains why there are many fine Japanese restaurants at almost all overseas destinations visited by large numbers of Japanese. These restaurants are usually owned and operated by Japanese companies, and they also cater to the local Japanese population. In fact, there are many Japanese restaurants in most big cities in the United States, Canada, Europe, Australia, Micronesia, New Zealand, Korea, Taiwan, Hong Kong, Singapore, and even South America.

Japanese favorites are sashimi, sushi, tempura, broiled fish, miso soup, pickled vegetables, and noodles. Many of the ingredients for these Japanese dishes are supplied locally, but others are flown in from Japan. Many of the chefs are on short-term assignments from their parent companies, but others have migrated to these countries to work there permanently. In some instances, Japanese food at overseas destinations is better and less expensive than that found in Japan. Main ingredients such as fresh fish, lobster, shrimp, crab, and clams are harvested locally. Older Japanese visitors particularly cannot part with their own customary diets, although most think they should try native cuisines. Many carry with them instant noodles, canned pickled vegetables, small soy sauce packages, pickled plums, and green tea bags when they ago abroad. Others may buy these items from local discount stores and supermarkets and take them to their hotel rooms to eat.

Teppan yaki (hot-plate cooking) is another favorite of many Japanese restaurant customers. The customers can choose from among such delicacies as beef, chicken, lobster, squids, oyster, fish, onions, green peppers, mushrooms, bean sprouts, zucchini, and garlic, and have the chef cook them at their table. Because the cooking is done before the customers, the food is fresh and tasty. In addition, almost all *teppan yaki* chefs demonstrate cooking theatricals and are quite entertaining. And the entire process from cooking to serving usually takes less than an hour, making it very popular among Japanese visitors with busy schedules. This type of cooking has become very popular among non-Japanese restaurant patrons in many parts of the world.

Italian Food

Young Japanese visitors enjoy Italian food, particularly spaghetti dishes. There are many Italian restaurants in big cities throughout Japan where patrons can taste a variety of Italian dishes. When Japanese visitors go to Italy, they are likely to go to famous Italian restaurants to taste authentic Italian cuisine and drink Italian wine.

French Food

There are many fine French restaurants in Japan. Major Western hotels have at least one French restaurant that caters to upscale hotel guests and other customers. Many Japanese chefs are trained in France, but the French dishes served in Japan are somewhat modified to suit Japanese taste. When Japanese visitors go to

France, they generally want to try authentic French cuisine with French wines at famous restaurants. Honeymooners and affluent middle-aged women in particular enjoy eating at a few of the most famous restaurants during their stay in Paris.

Alcoholic Beverages

Japanese visitors enjoy alcoholic beverages. They almost always drink during lunch and dinner. For lunch, they often drink a bottle of beer or wine; for dinner, their drinking routine usually begins with *kampai* (bottoms up) with a glass of beer, then a few glasses of *mizuwari* (scotch and water), then ends with a glass of fine brandy. Many Japanese men in particular order *sake* and drink it hot or on ice if they are eating Japanese food. *Shoochuu* (white liquor) is also popular among them. If they are visiting the Pacific islands, they may try a tropical drink, but they will quickly switch to beer or scotch whiskey. Japanese women also drink, but more moderately. They usually prefer sweeter drinks such as banana or strawberry daiquiris, gin fizzes, vodka tonics, piña coladas, and sweeter wines.

Most Japanese businessmen are heavy drinkers, since drinking is an important social activity when they are traveling together. They generally enjoy Scotch whiskeys, French brandies, American bourbons, and good wines. They also like locally brewed alcoholic beverages.

The legal drinking age in Japan is twenty, but most high school seniors and younger college students begin drinking before this age. This may present serious problems in foreign countries where the legal drinking age is twenty-one.

Behavior of Japanese Visitors in Restaurants

Eating and drinking behaviors are learned early in life. The proper behavior in Japan may look funny, peculiar, or even impolite in Western countries. It is difficult for Japanese visitors to instantly adapt to a different set of rules and learn proper etiquette when they go to foreign countries. There are several unique Japanese behaviors that need to be understood by restaurant managements and all levels of workers catering to Japanese customers.

Peculiar Japanese Behavior

Restaurant hosts and hostesses are often annoyed by Japanese visitors who show up at a restaurant without a reservation and expect to get a table right away. Sometimes they ignore the sign that says, "Please wait to be seated" and simply smile at the host or hostess and walk by. They may even rush and seat themselves at an empty table. Although rare, some Japanese visitors may try to sit at a table already taken by another person when they cannot find an empty table. Sitting with a stranger is called *aiseki* in Japanese, and it is done routinely in coffee shops during peak lunch or dinner hours. If one person seats himself at a larger table for four or more, the manager will politely ask the seated customer to share the same table with strangers. It seems that Japanese people are able to put invisible curtains in front of themselves, as customers sharing the same table usually ignore each other and do not engage in any conversation.

Many high-class Japanese-style or Western-style restaurants in Japan require advance reservations. But even these restaurants are usually prepared to take in a few walk-in customers. An astute manager will have a table or two set aside for important regular customers or demanding walk-ins. In Japan, it is very important for prominent persons such as top business executives, influential politicians, and famous movie stars to have a few restaurants where they can get a good table by simply walking in. For example, a top Japanese executive must entertain an important business associate from New York at a moment's notice. He will need the implicit arrangement with the managers of his favorite restaurants. For the executive, *kao ga kiku* (having strong personal influence) is very important, because this is a special privilege and something to be proud of. In other words, this executive can be demanding because of his high social status. In Japan, his name, job title, and company affiliation will have a strong impact on the type of treatment received. He may think he can make the same demands and receive the same respect even in foreign countries.

Seating and Service by Social Rank

Seating a group of Japanese visitors cannot be done randomly. Everyone in the group knows their own social status and ranking in relation to every other member. The main guest or highest ranking person is given *kamiza* (the honored seat), and the others are seated according to their relative status. *Kamiza* would be the center seat with a nice view of the garden, ocean, or mountain, and away from the entrance or walkway. The next best seat would be on the right of *kamiza,* and the third best seat is on the left. The highest-ranking person on the host's side is seated across the main guest. The second-ranking host is on the left, and the lowest-ranking person, who takes care of details such as ordering and paying the bill, sits closest to the door. (See the diagrams below.)

a. Japanese-style Room

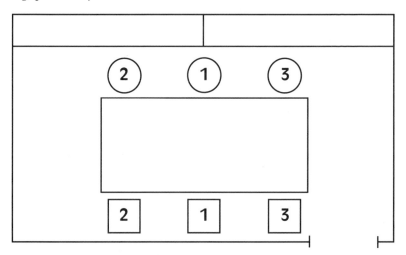

Note: A circle ○ indicates a guest; a square □ indicates a host.

b. Western-style Room

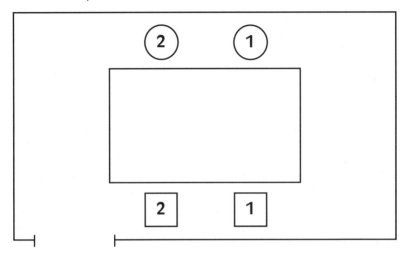

c. Chinese-style Room

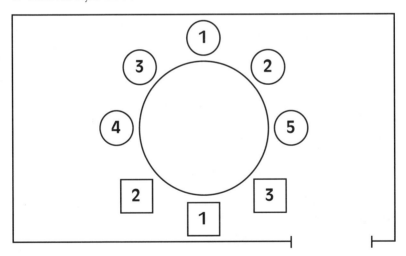

In most instances, main guests go through the social ritual of hesitating to take the honored seat right away. They politely refuse the offer a few times, but, in the end, they take the seat at the host's urging. When the main guests sit down, everyone else will find their assigned seats with the help of the host. The restaurant host in charge of the group should wait until this social maneuvering has finished before giving them menus.

Since Japan is traditionally a male-dominated society, male customers expect more attention and better service. Even though many young Japanese have begun to practice the Western courtesy of ladies first, it is not yet widely accepted by older Japanese visitors. In other words, cocktail and meal orders should be taken according to the social ranking of each person at the table. Again, drinks and meals should be served in order of social ranking. With older couples, wives will generally defer to their husbands and expect them to be served first. Restaurant hosts, waiters, and waitresses should not violate these Japanese social codes, because doing so would upset the honored guest and embarrass the host as well.

The Same Food and Drink for Everyone

Japanese tour group members tend to order the same food and drink rather than make different individual choices. There are several cultural reasons for this peculiar behavior. First, they want to taste *meibutsu* when they travel to a tourist destination. In Japan every city, town, or village has several nationally famous foods and drinks that every visitor expects to taste while visiting there. Consequently, Japanese visitors also want to look for *meibutsu* when they go to foreign destinations. For example, Japanese visitors to Hawaii feel that they must have Hawaiian tropical drinks such as the maitai, blue Hawaii, chichi, and okolehao, and local fishes such as mahimahi, onaga, and ono. They tend to follow the suggestion of the group leader as to what to order. If the group leader happens to be a high-ranking person and chooses a certain dish and drink, everyone else is obliged to follow him. And it is considered socially unacceptable for any group members of junior rank to order something more expensive than that of the leader.

Second, Japanese generally do not want to be bothered with making many different choices from an English language menu they may not fully understand. They may become confused and frustrated if they are asked what kind of beer, salad dressing, coffee, and dessert they would like to order. They frequently choose a complete dinner to avoid the cumbersome process of choosing single items as appetizer, soup, salad, entreé, and dessert. This is exactly the same way they order meals when dining in Japan. The Japanese are used to having all kinds of food and drinks, and they usually do not have strong likes or dislikes. A typical Japanese-style complete dinner includes raw fish, meat, poultry, and vegetables, served in small portions one after the other. In addition, a large variety of foods from all over the world is available in Japan today, and many Japanese visitors have tried semiauthentic foreign dishes and drinks in the past. One other important reason for this behavior is that Japanese religions generally do not impose strict religious taboos on food and drink. In the old days, Buddhism did not allow followers to eat animals because of the belief that their own ancestors may have been reincarnated as the animals that they might have slaughtered inadvertently. Buddhist monks were not allowed to eat either animals or fish centuries ago. But today Japanese people, including monks, eat meat and fish without worrying about religious taboos. In other words, it is easy to serve Japanese restaurant customers because they will eat virtually anything.

Quick and Efficient Service

Japanese people eat their meals very quickly compared to Westerners. Some Japanese customers may even get up and walk away before they are served a complete dinner. Because they are used to quick service in Japan, they often become impatient and frustrated with slow Western-style service. They are not used to spending two or three hours eating and socializing at the dinner table. In Japan, businessmen spend one hour and a half for dinner, then adjourn to a cocktail lounge for more socializing. This second outing is called *nijikai*. Young women may go to a coffee shop for more conversation. They may want to do the same when they go to a foreign country. Other Japanese restaurant customers, especially women, would rather rush through their meals and do more shopping.

Generally speaking, all Japanese customers would prefer to finish their breakfast in twenty minutes, lunch in thirty minutes, and dinner in one hour, because they are always on a very busy schedule. Restaurants at Japan's many tourist destinations offer a "tourist menu" with only a few selections of reasonably priced and good quality meals. The selections are either beef, pork, or fish dishes. These dishes are prepared in advance and served very efficiently. Because some of these dishes do not have to be served hot, Japanese restaurants usually place them on the tables shortly before a large group of customers arrive. This custom is another reason why hurried Japanese customers are frustrated with the slow and deliberate service at restaurants in foreign countries.

Unique Eating Manners

Western cuisine has always been very popular in Japan, but not all Japanese are familiar with proper Western table manners, hence some of them violate Western etiquette in eating and drinking. One Japanese habit that may disturb Westerners is the loud, slurping noise made when eating soup or noodles. In Japan, soup is served very hot, and it is not considered bad manners to blow on it and slurp it. Another Japanese habit is the practice of leaning over the table and eating with a knife in the right hand and fork in the left. Japanese may cut up an entire piece of steak at one time, then put a large piece into their mouths. Sometimes they raise the soup bowl or plate to their mouths. These are acceptable eating practices in Japan.

Some Japanese visitors exchange food with each other at the table, even in fine restaurants. Since sharing food is a gesture of friendship in Japan, they are always eager to exchange and taste others' selections. Some Japanese women almost always offer their husbands a portion of their dishes to show affection and concern. If this happens, the restaurant manager should not disapprove. Instead, the manager should have the waiter assist the diners by dividing up the food and providing extra dishes, forks, and napkins.

Another habit of many Japanese visitors, particularly older Japanese men, is the use of toothpicks at the table. This is considered bad manners in Western culture, but it is a very common and acceptable behavior in Japan. In fact, all restaurants in Japan keep a toothpick holder on every table, along with a small bottle of soy sauce and salt and pepper shakers.

Noisy Merrymaking and Poor Tipping

The Japanese are generally shy and quiet people. But after having a few drinks with a group of people, they can become quite bold and noisy. For them, becoming intoxicated is a good excuse to engage in loud and active conversation. Some Japanese men use this as an excuse to tease the young waitresses serving them. They may start shouting to one another and even start singing loudly. This type of merrymaking can be a real annoyance for non-Japanese patrons of the restaurant, especially when the noisemakers are speaking only in Japanese. In Japan, an *enkai* (drinking party) of more than five people is ordinarily held in a private room so that the noisy patrons will not disturb others in the restaurant. To accommodate drinking parties, large Japanese restaurants have many private rooms of different sizes. If a restaurant does not have any private rooms, there could be problems in accommodating and pleasing these large parties.

Poor tipping is another common complaint from waiters and waitresses who must depend on tips for additional income. In Japan, fine dining restaurants routinely add a 10 percent service charge to each check in lieu of tipping. In coffee shops and family restaurants, customers are not expected to leave any tips. Many Japanese customers think that the tipping custom is the same in other countries as it is in Japan. Sometimes they simply forget to tip, even though tour brochures and guidebooks advise them on tipping customs in Western countries.

But even in Japan there are some situations that require tipping. At a Japanese inn where dinner is served in the guests' room, it is necessary to give maids in charge a small envelope with money enclosed when they come to greet the guests right after the check-in. In Japan, it is extremely impolite to give money openly, as it is done in Western countries. And the amount of the tip will influence service to be received. At geisha parties *maiko* dancers, singer-musicians, and even waitresses will receive small envelopes with money enclosed from the host before they start serving the guests. Hostesses at cocktail lounges expect to receive tips as well. The problem is that the Japanese are not used to tipping to everyone who serves them under all circumstances.

In order to avoid unpleasant squabbles over tipping, Japanese tour wholesalers usually include a 15 percent tip on all meal coupons. Some Japanese restaurants, with the consent of customers, routinely add a 15 percent tip to the amount of the check. The waiter or waitress can ask politely if they may include a 15 percent service fee. Still other restaurants put large stamped messages on every check in Japanese: *Chippu wa fukumarete imasen* (Gratuities are not included). No matter how Japanese restaurant customers handle tipping, it would be in poor taste for employees to demand tips. In fact, in Japan it is almost a social crime to show open disgust or disrespect when customers unintentionally fail to tip for restaurant service.

Promotion of Good Food Service

Until recently many fine Western-style restaurants catered mainly to English-speaking customers. With the influx of affluent Japanese visitors, these restaurants have had to make several adjustments in order to provide better service to these "nontraditional" customers. They have begun printing bilingual menus, hiring Japanese-speaking waiters and waitresses, and holding Japanese language and culture classes for the entire staff. Japanese customers have high expectations regarding the quality of food and service, as they come from a country where they generally receive superb food service. Restaurants should take specific steps to respond to the needs and wishes of Japanese visitors if they wish to develop and maintain good business with them.

Bilingual Menus

Printing bilingual menus is the first step for restaurants in overcoming communication problems. Because many Japanese visitors do not speak English and are not familiar with Western-style food service, good bilingual menus are very important in increasing their patronage. Any menu translation should be done by professionals familiar with technical food service terms and expressions in both English and Japanese. Many food and beverage names in English cannot be translated literally into Japanese. Some English, French, or Italian names for certain dishes cannot be translated at all because there are no equivalent dishes in Japan. These are simply transcribed in *katakana* syllables based on Japanese pronunciation. For example, menu, appetizer, cocktail, whiskey, beer, juice, and rice are written as *menyuu, apetaizaa, kakuteru, uisukii, biiru, juusu,* and *raisu.* However, non-Japanese speaking waiters and waitresses may have difficulty understanding them if Japanese customers pronounce these loanwords as written. To solve this problem some restaurants have devised a numbering system, and some others now insert color pictures of the most popular dishes. Many seafood restaurants show what they serve by keeping live lobsters, crabs, shrimp, and fish in saltwater tanks in clear view of restaurant customers. Some restaurants display several different fish, fresh oysters and clams, cuts of chilled steaks, lamb, and pork on beds of crushed ice in the dining area. These displays are effective visual menus for Japanese customers who do not speak English.

One problem with large printed bilingual menus is that they cannot include information on specials of the day, which are usually recited by the waiter. It would be good policy to offer a Japanese translation of these specials on a separate sheet or have a Japanese-speaking host explain them. This extra consideration could generate more income, as specials are usually higher priced than regular menu items. Japanese customers would undoubtedly be more satisfied because they could then have fresh fish, excellent chilled meats, good poultry, or seasonal vegetables that are served as "today's specials."

Some restaurants give Japanese customers smaller Japanese language menus with only several dishes, including favorites of Japanese customers. This abbreviated menu has both advantages and disadvantages. The advantages are (1) the customers do not have to struggle with big menus that present too many choices; (2) the waiter or waitress does not have to explain menu items; and (3) the restaurant can save on the cost of printing a large bilingual menu, and any revisions could be done at minimal cost. On the other hand, the disadvantages are (1) customers cannot order dishes not included in the smaller menu; (2) some customers may even suspect they are being discriminated against and charged more, simply because they cannot speak English; (3) the restaurant cannot satisfy repeat customers wishing to order a variety of different dishes on each visit; and (4) bilingual Japanese customers will probably be upset if they are given the "menu for Japanese tourists."

Extra Personal Attention

A little extra attention and kindness extended to Japanese customers goes a long way. A sincere attitude, friendly smile, and prompt action are extremely important in serving any guest. Japanese visitors often judge restaurant service by the nonverbal behavior of the staff rather than on their verbal behavior. The "why can't you speak English" attitude can be detected easily by customers. In some instances, the staff may speak English to Japanese customers very slowly and deliberately when they discover that the customers cannot speak English. But those who can speak English may become infuriated if they are spoken to in this fashion.

Waiters and waitresses who cannot speak Japanese may pretend to not recognize Japanese customers' requests and look away, then head for English-speaking customers. Perhaps they feel unable to help them or expect someone else who does speak Japanese to handle customers' requests. Whatever the excuses they may have, such avoidance behavior would definitely insult the customers and in turn would hurt the restaurant's business. Another problem occurs when waiters or waitresses have private conversations in English while looking or pointing at Japanese customers. Customers would probably sense they are being talked about and feel that they are being ridiculed. Such impolite and disrespectful behavior would be detrimental to the restaurant's reputation and business. On the other hand, a sincere smile, not an artificial one, is important in communicating willingness and enthusiasm to provide good service. A smile would certainly help promote goodwill and a good image.

The most serious problem in providing prompt service to Japanese customers could be related to the strict division of labor based on job descriptions. Especially in unionized restaurants in the United States, there are several job categories among restaurant workers: busboy, waiter/waitress, cocktail server, sommelier, host/hostess, bartender. All employees are expected to work strictly according to their job descriptions. It would be a serious violation of the union contract if someone were to do another person's job. Restaurant management cannot force any union worker to perform tasks not included in the job description.

This type of situation would not help if a restaurant were full of impatient Japanese customers. For example, if a group of Japanese customers wishes to order drinks, they could not ask the waiter or waitress to take cocktail orders. Instead, they would have to wait for a cocktail server to come and take orders. If they would like to order more drinks later, they would have to wait again for the cocktail server to return. Later, if one customer wanted to have a bottle of wine, the cocktail server would have to ask a sommelier to take the order. In the meantime, the customers would be subjected to a long wait for service.

This situation would never happen in Japan because a manager may assign other workers immediately without causing any trouble with the labor union. Restaurants should recognize that under certain circumstances flexible work rules and teamwork on the part of all workers is necessary to promote good business with Japanese customers. Union work rules should not be made absolute in situations like this.

Meal Coupons

Accepting meal coupons or vouchers issued by Japanese tour wholesalers is an effective way to ensure constant business from Japanese visitors. Wholesalers offer package tours with or without meals. Most likely, Japanese visitors who buy deluxe tour packages with meals are first-time travelers with more money to spend. They will go to the restaurants of their hotels and other upscale restaurants designated by the tour wholesaler. In contrast, those who buy less expensive tour packages are either repeaters or low-budget travelers. They tend to go to coffee shops, fast-food restaurants, convenience stores, or family restaurants.

Meal coupons are issued by tour wholesalers based on a contractual agreement with participating restaurants. The coupons are very convenient for Japanese visitors who cannot speak English and those who find it too troublesome to order and pay for meals on their own. Each coupon is good for a complete meal whether it is breakfast, lunch, or dinner. The coupon itself does not have a face value, but it states several choices of dishes and specific restaurants where the coupon may be used. It also explains in Japanese how to use it. For example, a coupon for one complete dinner at a hotel restaurant in Hawaii may include one tropical drink, one appetizer, a main dish, dessert, coffee or tea, local tax, and a 15 percent gratuity

There are two major reasons why Japanese tour wholesalers still market meal coupons. One is to generate good revenue from selling these coupons with package tours. Another is to ensure that their clients will be served good meals and receive extra courtesy. Tour wholesalers, with cooperation from their local tour operators, carefully choose the restaurants. Because they will be held responsible for any mistreatment, food poisoning, or even minor accidents, they must check on the food, the beverages, the service, the ambience, and the management of each restaurant before negotiating a contract. The contract will specify menu selections, prices, payment schedule, and other conditions. When the net price of each meal is agreed upon, the tour wholesalers add their own markup and decide the retail price of each meal coupon. The percentage of the markup depends on the types of meal packages, the kinds of restaurants, the volume of business, and other factors.

For participating restaurants, there is another major advantage in accepting meal coupons. Since Japanese customers with meal coupons generally order one or two of the preordered complete meals, say steak and lobster or the seafood combination platter, the restaurant would know in advance what and how many meals will be sold each evening. The waiters can serve the customers quickly without having to ask many questions. For example, twenty Japanese honeymoon couples come in for dinner and all have the steak and lobster and the same tropical drink. The honeymooners probably would not complain about the quick service because they are used to being served this way in Japan. In fact, they would probably be happy to finish the complete meal in less than an hour and then go out shopping or dancing. Because the restaurant could expect a quick turnover of tables, it will be possible to serve many other guests during the same evening.

Undoubtedly, accepting meal coupons can be a lucrative business for many participating restaurants.

Recently, many Japanese honeymooners have begun to go to plush seafood restaurants for deluxe meals with limousine transfers. This deluxe dinner package is again arranged by tour wholesalers as a part of the ever-popular deluxe honeymoon tours.

Chapter 7

Shopping Habits and Souvenir Merchandising

Japanese visitors are well known for their shopping sprees at tourist destinations around the world. Shopping is one of the most popular pastimes of Japanese visitors of all ages. Wherever they go on sightseeing trips in Japan, they still practice the age-old custom of buying *omiyage* (souvenirs) for relatives, friends, coworkers, superiors, subordinates, business associates, and neighbors. Souvenir giving is the most common method of cultivating and nurturing amicable interpersonal relationships and showing appreciation to those with whom one lives and works. Japanese travelers will do the same when they take overseas trips. This social custom undoubtedly makes them the best customers for the many tourist shops and retail stores catering to them.

Store owners, managers, and sales clerks must understand the unique cultural and economic reasons behind Japanese visitors' shopping habits. They should learn why these visitors can afford to buy so many souvenirs, why they buy particular items, and why they prefer to go to certain stores. They should also learn appropriate sales approaches and tactics if they wish to be successful in selling to Japanese customers.

Senbetsu (Monetary Gifts) and *Omiyage* (Souvenirs)

According to a recent survey, affluent Japanese visitors spend an average of three thousand dollars per person on souvenirs when they go to foreign countries. Even younger Japanese office workers spend at least one thousand dollars on their overseas vacation trips. There are several cultural reasons why they buy so many souvenirs. Whenever Japanese people travel overseas on vacation or even on business, they usually receive *senbetsu* from their family members, relatives, friends, and coworkers. When they receive these gifts, they are obligated to buy an appropriate souvenir in return. The value and type of souvenir for any particular person is determined primarily by the amount of their monetary gift and the nature of the relationship with the traveler. Japanese honeymooners who have received a lot of money from their in-laws are obligated to buy expensive brand-name souvenirs that are sure to be appreciated. But for their own parents, they may get by with less expensive souvenirs or token gifts, even though they might have received much more money from them. Honeymooners usually prepare a long list of souvenirs that they must not forget to buy, because they receive monetary gifts from many other people. An office clerk may receive money from several coworkers who actually request certain items. A young college student who has received a lot of money from his or her parents and grandparents may buy a token gift for each of them. A junior manager who has received some money from a senior manager should buy an expensive souvenir that costs more than the amount of money given to him. In a nutshell, receiving *senbetsu* creates a strong social obligation to buy *omiyage*. This is one of the most important reasons why Japanese visitors spend so many hours shopping on overseas trips.

Souvenirs Given with Ulterior Motives

Buying favors with lavish gifts has been an established social practice among the Japanese for centuries. They routinely use appropriate gifts to communicate a wide range of unspoken messages to the recipients. (In this case *senbetsu* is usually not given.) In fact, a souvenir from abroad can be an excellent gift to curry favor. A Japanese businessman may buy an expensive set of American golf clubs for an important client who is a golf enthusiast in order to cement a pending business deal. A junior executive who is up for promotion in a few months may purchase for his superior a bottle of very expensive Napoleon brandy and implicitly solicit the latter's support. A department head may buy small boxes of chocolate candies for all of his subordinates to show appreciation for their hard work during his absence. Or a housewife who has asked a neighbor to watch her house will buy the neighbor a small gift to show appreciation. This last form of gift is called *orei* (a token of appreciation).

Another form of gift giving is called *okaeshi* (return gift). The social etiquette of returning a gift requires that the initial recipient return the favor at an appropriate time in the future. The return gift, however, should be of equal value or preferably slightly more than the value of the gift received earlier. For example, a senior citizen visitor gave a neighbor a box of Hawaiian papaya upon returning from Hawaii. A few months later, when this neighbor goes to Hawaii, he or she would be expected to return the favor by bringing a box of Hawaiian papaya and a box of chocolate-covered macadamia nuts. If the neighbor fails to do so, it would be a clear violation of the traditional social custom of reciprocal gift giving. This practice of receiving and returning of gifts may continue almost indefinitely as long as both parties wish to maintain a cordial interpersonal relationship.

Most Popular Souvenir Items

Foreign-made items have always been popular with the Japanese. Throughout its modern history Japan has borrowed much from Europe and the United States. Even today when made-in-Japan products are of equal or superior quality, Japanese still tend to regard foreign-made items as more prestigious and very fashionable. Japanese women prefer French perfumes, European fashions, French or Italian shoes, and handbags. Japanese men tend to like Swiss watches, Scotch whiskeys, Italian shoes, French neckties, and English fabrics for business suits. Some Western sociologists speculate that this peculiar preference for foreign items might be a reflection of the deep-seated inferiority complex that the Japanese have had toward Western civilization for centuries. Others explain that this unusual behavior is a means of satisfying the vanity of those Japanese people who cannot afford to buy their own homes. They want to fantasize that they are "rich" by wearing expensive foreign-made items.

A more practical reason for buying souvenirs overseas is that they can be purchased at much lower prices in foreign countries. Despite the fact that the Japanese government has relaxed import regulations and reduced tariffs, imported goods are still expensive due to inefficient marketing systems and the monopolistic agency agreements controlled by large trading companies and wholesalers. In fact, Japanese women can purchase French cosmetics in Hawaii at less than half the price in Japan. Japanese men can buy Scotch whiskeys or Swiss watches at bargain prices at duty-free shops at any overseas destination. The recent drastic appreciation of the Japanese yen against major world currencies, especially against the U.S. dollar, also makes it much more advantageous for visitors to buy things overseas.

Furthermore, the most important reason for spending a lot of time and money on foreign products is that they must buy "real" *omiyage*. *Omiyage* actually refers to any locally grown or manufactured article that is well known as a desirable souvenir form a particular town, region, or country. At every visitor destination in Japan, souvenir shops carry hundreds of items ranging from carved wooden dolls, handicrafts, pickled vegetables, cakes, *sake*, green tea, and seasonal fruits, to neckties, tie tacks, pearls, and *kimono*. Most of the lobby area in all Japanese inns in hot-spring resorts is used for showcases displaying a large number of these souvenirs. All items are labeled with the place of origin and are packed with a small pamphlet explaining where and how they were made. Almost all Shinto shrines and Buddhist temples in Japan sell amulets and other sacred items as souvenirs to worshippers and visitors.

The problem with many souvenirs, however, is that almost all those that are sold in the United States, Canada, Australia, and Europe are imported from newly industrialized countries such as Korea, Taiwan, Hong Kong, the Philippines, Thailand, and more recently from China. Imported items are generally not appreciated by Japanese visitors because they are not considered good souvenirs. Retail store management should recognize what *omiyage* means to the Japanese and should make every effort to stock "true" souvenirs for them.

Generally speaking, the most popular souvenir items are liquor, cigarettes, perfume, jewelry, watches, cigarette lighters, pens, neckties and tie tacks, bags, shoes, leather goods, sports equipment, clothing, fruits, and other food items.

Liquor

Many Japanese men are heavy drinkers. Since they usually drink alcoholic beverages for all kinds of occasions, foreign brandies, whiskeys, bourbons, and wines are considered desirable souvenirs. Japanese visitors are allowed to bring home three bottles of liquor duty free. (Minors are not allowed to bring in liquor, even for their parents' use.) For souvenirs, they will usually buy expensive brandies or Scotch whiskeys. They also buy favorite high-quality whiskeys at duty-free shops for their own consumption because these superior Scotch whiskeys are prohibitively expensive in Japan.

The most popular whiskeys are Chivas Regal, Old Parr, Dimple, Johnnie Walker, Jack Daniels, and Wild Turkey. Popular brandies are Camus Napoleon, Remy Martin, Chateau Beaulon, Courvoisier, and Chabot. Wines from various famous wine-making countries are becoming popular these days. Japanese visitors to France, Australia, New Zealand, Switzerland, Germany, Italy, Spain, Canada, and the United States usually buy wines from these countries. Today, drinking imported wine has become a particularly popular activity among young businesswomen. Many men who visit China buy special rice wines with certain medicinal effects.

Some Japanese businessmen willingly spend one thousand dollars or more for one expensive bottle of French cognac for an important client. Many affluent businessmen even show off a collection of rare and expensive foreign liquors in glass showcases in their offices or living rooms. Some whiskeys come in uniquely shaped bottles such as the annual Hawaiian Open Golf Tournament commemorative bottle and golf club head–shaped containers designed for golf enthusiasts. Bottles like these are collectors' items, and the contents are rarely consumed.

Cigarettes

Although many countries, particularly the United States, encourage people not to smoke, Japanese people are still smoking a lot of cigarettes. Many men are chain smokers, and even some young women have begun smoking. Until recently Japan's cigarette industry was controlled by government monopoly, and imported cigarettes have always been more expensive than domestic brands. Due to strong political pressure from the United States, the prices of imported American cigarettes have come down considerably in recent years. Like imported liquor, foreign cigarettes are considered more prestigious and desirable. The most popular American cigarettes are Marlboro, Lark, Winston, Kent, Camel, Benson & Hedges, and Philip Morris because these brands are familiar to Japanese smokers. European cigarettes such as Dunhill, John Player Special, Cartier, Courreges, Manchester Classic, and Zino Davidoff are considered more desirable. The normal duty-free allowance is two cartons of cigarettes or fifty cigars.

Perfumes and Other Cosmetics

French perfumes are a most prized souvenir among many Japanese women, not only because they are still very expensive in Japan, but also because they are much more prestigious. Famous brand name perfumes such as Nina Ricci, Chanel, Christian Dior(the three best known in Japan), Guerlain, Hermes, Guy Larouche, Van Cleef & Arpel, Jean Desprez, Givenchy, Ralph Lauren, Jean Patou, Dunhill, Cartier, and Yves Saint Laurent are very popular. Japanese citizens are allowed to bring home two ounces (four half-ounce bottles) of perfume duty free.

Other cosmetics such as lipsticks, face creams, eye shadows, and hair care products of the above brand names are also popular as souvenirs. American cosmetic products made by Clinique, Estee Lauder, Max Factor, and Revlon are becoming popular among young Japanese women, who often buy these products for themselves. Some economy-minded Japanese shoppers may buy a year's supply of less expensive products for themselves and their friends.

Jewelry

Traditionally Japanese people have had a strong interest in fine jewelry. Now that most Japanese have larger disposable incomes, they are buying more gold, platinum, and other fine gems on overseas trips. Because Japan does not have any gold, silver, diamond, or other gemstone mines within its national boundaries, all precious metals and gems must be imported. This is the major reason why fine jewelry is much more expensive in Japan. The complex multilayer distribution channels of fine jewelry also add to the cost of these items.

Diamonds, emeralds, sapphires, rubies, opals, lapis, jades, topazes, and amethysts are favorites of Japanese shoppers. According to a recent survey by a major jeweler in Hawaii, purchase of solitaire diamonds of around $5,000 is quite common among middle-aged women. Diamond earrings and pendants around $500 to $2,000 are popular among young women. Precious stones mounted on platinum, white gold, and 18k gold settings are very popular. (Japanese people do not like gold items under 18k, which is the standard in Japan.) Rings, necklaces, earrings, gold chains, and pearls priced under $350 are popular among Japanese shoppers of all ages.

Japanese visitors naturally look for local products when they buy fine jewelry and gems. Many Japanese visitors to Hong Kong feel they should buy fine jewelry since they know they can find good bargains. Those who visit Australia may buy opals native to Australia. Visitors to Hawaii, Guam, Saipan, and other tropical islands in the Pacific generally purchase coral jewelry. The most popular ones are pink, gold, or black coral necklaces, pendants, rings, earrings, tie tacks, and cuff links. In some instances, Japanese women may buy expensive diamonds and give them to their daughters or daughters-in-law as family heirlooms.

Watches

Although Japanese watches are excellent, Japanese people still like to buy famous Swiss watches. Sometimes affluent Japanese businessmen buy expensive Swiss watches to show off and impress their associates and friends.

Omega and Rolex watches are the most popular among Japanese businessmen. Other popular designer watches are Ebel, Cartier, Hermes, Dunhill, Bally, Longines, Piaget, Rado, Issot, Hever, Tiffany, Carrera y Carrera, and Charles Jourdan. Japanese citizens are allowed to bring in one watch for personal use if it is within the duty-free allowance of $2,000. Another incentive for buying fine watches abroad is that the watches are taxed on the import price (generally 60 percent of the market price) rather than the retail price paid. For example, if a Japanese visitor paid $10,000 for a Cartier watch at a retail shop, he or she will pay the duty on 60 percent, or $6,000 of the retail value.

Cigarette Lighters and Pens

Famous name-brand cigarette lighters such as Dunhill, Dupont, and Cartier are high-status accessories among Japanese smokers. Both men and women smokers like to discreetly show off their expensive lighters. They are willing to pay several hundred dollars for a famous brand for this purpose. They also buy expensive ball-point pens for souvenirs and their own use. The most popular pens are Sheaffer, Cross, Valentino, Pierre Cardin, and Mont Blanc pens. An expensive set of Mont Blanc pens is considered an excellent gift for top executives. Because these lighters and pens are more likely to be used every day by the recipients, these gifts can be good reminders of on-going business relationships.

Neckties and Tie Tacks

Neckties have always been considered good gifts for Japanese men. Well-groomed men wear good neckties when they go to work. In the Japanese cultural context, wearing an expensive brand-name necktie is a sign of good personal taste and high social status. Businessmen are willing to spend $150 or more for a pure silk French or Italian necktie. They prefer well-known designer neckties such as Dunhill, Dupont, Christian Dior, Gucci, Hermes, Longchamps, Regent Club, Yves Saint Laurent, Polo, and Bally. Choosing a good necktie as a souvenir is very important for both male and female shoppers. (Japanese women are expected to know the taste and preference of their husbands and buy suitable neckties for them.)

Tie tacks are also popular gift items. Fashion-conscious Japanese men may wear Dunhill neckties and matching Dunhill tie tacks and cuff links. Most brand-name necktie makers have their own tie tack and cuff link sets for loyal customers.

Many Japanese companies and schools give away neckties, tie tacks, and cuff links with their logos for promotional purposes. In some instances, these items are distributed to commemorate the opening or anniversary of these organizations. They are also given to important visitors as souvenirs because they are good mementos.

Handbags, Shoes, and Other Leather Goods

No large-scale leather goods manufacturing industry has ever flourished in Japan because Buddhist teachings condemned the slaughter of animals and the making of leather goods. Japan has always depended on importing leather goods from other countries. Today, the Japanese buy all kinds of high-quality leather goods when they travel overseas. They find that these foreign-made leather goods are less expensive and more desirable as compared to those found at home.

Many young Japanese women like to buy designer bags made by Chanel, Louis Vuitton, Gucci, Christian Dior, Dooney & Bourke, Celine, Comtesse, Cartier, Renoma, Courreges, Gold Pfeil, Nina Ricci, and Etro. Designer bags have apparently become status symbols among young office workers, and they are willing to spend more than one thousand dollars to buy one of these bags in order to join the ranks of fashion-conscious young women. Many also buy leather shoes (mostly for their own use) because the shoes are of higher quality and are comparatively inexpensive.

Many Japanese men buy leather belts for their own use and as souvenirs. The most popular are by Christian Dior, Givenchy, Bally, Longchamps, Dunhill, Lancel, Celine, and Renoma. They are suitable as small gifts for friends and relatives because they are less expensive than other items. Many men also buy shoes for themselves if they can find the right sizes. (Japanese men tend to have wider and shorter feet, and EE and EEE sizes are very common.) The most popular brands are Bally, Sperry Topsiders, Ferragamo, Charles Jourdan, and Cole Haan. Some even purchase cowboy boots, hats, and leather jackets just for the fun of owning them. More affluent Japanese businessmen buy Dunhill or Louis Vuitton golf bags to impress their business associates and fellow golfers.

Sports Equipment and Clothing

Western sports such as golf, tennis, baseball, basketball, soccer, surfing, and windsurfing have become very popular in Japan. Japanese visitors, particularly sports-minded young men, are always looking for something that will enhance their skills in their favorite sport. For example, golf enthusiasts might look for special drivers or putters that will presumably improve their golf scores. Avid tennis players might hunt for the newest tennis rackets to help improve their serves.

Golf and tennis wear with logos are also very popular. Young Japanese men often purchase logo shirts, caps, and jackets of American professional golfers, major league baseball teams, National Football League teams, National Basketball Association teams, and T-shirts with pictures of world-famous sports figures. Japanese high school and college students enjoy wearing T-shirts and torn designer jeans, just like American students.

Fruits and Other Food Items

In Japan, food has always been considered the most desirable gift. One prized gift is *hatsumono* (the very first crop) of good fruits when they are still rare and very expensive. *Hatsumono* of cherries, white peaches, grapes, melons, oranges, apples, and persimmons are the most desirable gifts. In recent years, rare fruits not grown in Japan have become popular gifts among the Japanese. Apparently they have come to like the fruits they tasted on overseas trips. For example, Hawaiian papaya and pineapples, California oranges, New Zealand kiwis, Malaysian mangosteen, and Mexican mangoes have become popular gift items in Japan.

Frozen or chilled American and Australian beef, beef jerky, live Maine lobsters, live Dungeness crabs, Alaskan smoked salmon, chocolate-covered macadamia nuts, roasted macadamia nuts, gourmet coffee beans, gourmet ice cream, American cookies, jams, cashew nuts, almonds, and Canadian maple syrup are high on the souvenir lists of many Japanese visitors. Many of these food items are unreasonably expensive in Japan despite the increasing pressure by consumers to lower prices.

Attractive Stores

"Japanese tour groups are herded into a few Japanese-owned gift shops. Local businesses cannot receive any benefit from the Japanese tourist trade at all!" This is a common complaint of store owners who are unable to attract Japanese customers. This attitide indicates that they are not familiar with unique Japanese social customs and cultural factors in retail merchandising and selling. Naturally, Japanese will shop in the same manner as they do in Japan and look for similar stores and expect the same service. They shop at famous specialty stores, souvenir shops, airport shops, duty-free shops, in-flight shops, souvenir vendors, and discount stores.

Famous Specialty Stores

Japanese visitors prefer to shop at famous specialty stores, even though they know that the prices at such stores may be higher than at other stores. They tend to believe that these stores carry higher-quality merchandise. Young Japanese visitors wish to gain a sense of belonging to an elite, affluent class by shopping at world-famous stores. They will buy one or two items there and then tell their friends and relatives about their shopping experiences. They may also carry around the shopping bags, showing off famous logos to others.

Specialty stores are called *senmonten* in Japanese. Western-style hotels in Japan generally have one or two floors of shopping arcades lined with specialty stores. These stores offer a wide variety of goods such as jewelry, clothing, leather goods, books, electronics, cameras, and sundries. Today many department stores have floors of designer merchandise sales sections. The menswear floors may have separate areas for Freeman, Barberry, Yves Saint Laurent, Calvin Klein, Valentino Garavani, Ralph Lauren, Chester Barrier, Polo, Benetton, and many others. Women's wear sections include Christian Dior, Gres, Hardy Amies, Perrer Balmain, Valentino Garavani, Allister Blair, Victor Edelstein, Chanel, Lanvin, Givenchy, Bruce Oldfield, Basile, Liz Claiborne, and Benetton. Frequent shoppers at these specialty stores will usually try to find the same items at overseas stores and will buy them if the prices, quality, and styles are better than those to be found in Japan.

Souvenir Shops

Souvenir shops are called *omiyageten,* and they cater almost exclusively to out of town visitors. These shops have ample parking spaces for large tour buses, passenger vans, limousines, and taxis. All Japanese tour wholesalers make certain that all of their tour groups stop at these souvenir shops during transfers and sightseeing trips. Tour escorts and bus drivers encourage tour members to buy by recommending famous souvenirs and good buys at each store. In return, the shops pay rebates to their companies. In most cases, the tour escorts and bus drivers are compensated personally if they make an extra effort to push the purchase of more souvenirs. The shops usually have a waiting lounge for them where they can enjoy tea, coffee, and snacks.

Most of the merchandise sold at souvenir shops can be either locally manufactured articles well known in that particular region or inexpensive imported trinkets. There are a wide variety of items such as wood carvings, handicrafts, china, clothing, footwear, candies, cookies, canned nuts, toys, paintings, and sundries. All food items have expiration dates stamped on the outside of the packaging. Many of these items are prepacked or prewrapped with the store's logo and are ready to be handed to customers because their shopping stops are usually fifteen minutes or so.

Airport Shops

Japanese visitors often go to airport shops to do last-minute shopping for souvenirs. Because many of them like to use up leftover foreign currency, they will think of something else to buy at the airport. They may visit every shop in the airport lobby. Unlike many passengers from Western countries, Japanese passengers generally do not wait by simply sitting around and quietly reading newspapers or magazines.

Duty-Free Shops

Duty-free shops located at major tourist destinations around the world have a virtual monopoly on Japanese shoppers. A vast majority of Japanese travelers never fail to visit duty-free shops on their overseas trips. Because Japanese importers and wholesalers seem to have established informal "cartels" among themselves, popular imported items such as liquor, cigarettes, precious metals, gems, cosmetics, and other luxury items are still more expensive in Japan. At duty-free shops, almost all Japanese shoppers buy whiskeys, cigarettes, and perfume. Many of them also buy expensive Swiss watches, leather goods, diamonds, gold rings, necklaces, bracelets, neckties, belts, and other foreign-made items.

All duty-free shops work very closely with Japanese tour wholesalers, local tour operators, tour guides, and tour drivers. Not only do the duty-free shops have an agreement with them on commission payments, but they also promise to provide excellent customer service to their clients. Major duty-free shops have customer service centers in key tourist-generating cities in Japan to handle customer complaints and to maintain good customer relations.

These shops issue an *okaimono kaado* (shopping card) to all shoppers. This is their identification card, which includes the shopper's flight number, departure date, and tour company's identification number. The shops record all purchases made by particular shoppers and send commission checks to the shoppers' tour companies. Major tour companies can receive a large monthly commission check, if they send all of their tour members to the duty-free shops. This system applies not only to the tour group members, but also to individual customers as long as they can identify their tour company. These shops also provide a comfortable waiting lounge for tour guides and tour drivers where they can enjoy refreshments, snacks, and even meals. They sponsor Christmas parties, picnics, and golf tournaments for tour company managers and employees in order to entice them to send more shoppers. They have Japanese-speaking salesclerks and customer service managers who are always ready to cater to the Japanese customers' needs. They have long business hours, usually from 9:00 A.M. to 10:00 P.M., for the convenience of Japanese shoppers who may come after dinner shows or all-day sightseeing. During peak holiday travel periods such as New Year's and Golden Week, they will remain open until midnight to accommodate the holiday crowds. Some duty-free shops even provide free limousine service for late-night shoppers.

In addition, most of these shops own and operate nonduty-free souvenir shops at the same location or at other locations. These souvenir shops again work with Japanese tour wholesalers, local tour operators, tour guides, and tour drivers. They have the same commission agreement with tour companies, which enables them to capture an equal number of Japanese shoppers who would otherwise buy nonduty-free items at other souvenir shops. For example, DFS in Hawaii has one floor for nonduty-free souvenir items in the same Waikiki building that houses its duty-free shop on other floors. In addition, DFS operates another duty-free shop and several souvenir shops at the Honolulu International Airport. Typically tour buses, vans, and limousines stop at all these tourist shops on the way to the hotels in Waikiki and depart for the airport a few hours early so that the passengers can have ample time to shop before departure.

In-Flight Shops

All international airlines offer in-flight shopping for the convenience of their passengers, although merchandise selections are limited. They sell liquor, cigarettes, perfume, jewelry, scarves, neckties, and other duty-free items on board. Japanese passengers who have forgotten to purchase some of these items will usually buy them, as they must fulfill the social obligation to bring home enough souvenirs. Busy businessmen are more likely to use in-flight shopping, as they probably did not have time to shop before departure.

Another variation on in-flight shopping is catalog sales of a wide variety of merchandise from all over the world. It is easy for airlines to sell them because they fly to many foreign countries from which these goods are harvested, grown, or manufactured. For example, Japan Airlines' catalog on trans-Pacific flights includes fresh California oranges, live Maine lobsters, smoked Alaskan salmon, Hawaiian pineapples and papayas, Mexican mangoes, Singapore orchids, and many other gift items. All purchases are paid for by credit card, and goods are shipped to the passengers' addresses in Japan. Japan Airline logo items such as garment bags, attaché cases, and golf bags seem to be popular among Japanese passengers who like "airline fashions."

Souvenir Vendors

All tour wholesalers and local tour operators engage in the souvenir sales business because it brings a substantial profit to them. Major tour wholesalers have their own subsidiary companies specializing in this business. They print large souvenir catalogs by major destinations with colorful and attractive pictures of many native products. The catchphrase of this service is, "You can enjoy your vacation time by reserving your *omiyage* before your departure. We will deliver them to your home at the same time of your arrival!" The message is, "Don't waste your vacation time by hunting for *omiyage*. Leave everything to us." Indeed, these companies can provide for customers the convenience of not having to buy and carry souvenirs themselves. Since the average Japanese visitor has only three or four full days for sightseeing, sports activities, and shopping, they are usually willing to pay higher prices to save time. Smaller tour companies also engage local souvenir vendors to supply merchandise and provide delivery service.

There are two types of delivery service: merchandise delivery to the airport and merchandise delivery to a home in Japan. For the first service, each tour member must fill out the airport delivery *omiyage* application blank. The list includes more than fifty different items, ranging from chocolate-covered macadamia nuts, ice cream, nuts, flowers and fruits, beef jerky, seafood, steaks, coffees, and cookies, to golf balls, gift sets, and liquor. Customers pay for whatever items they have chosen in advance. The goods are then delivered to the airport check-in counter at the time of the passenger's departure. He or she will confirm with the airport representative all of the goods purchased and will receive airline baggage claim checks for them. Upon arrival in Japan, the passenger will claim them and then go through customs.

For the second delivery service, customers must fill in the Japan delivery *omiyage* application blank and all purchases will then be shipped to Japan and delivered to their residence. Prices are naturally much higher for this service, but the customer need not do anything except pay for the purchases. The tour company will do everything else, including clearing customs and shipping. To provide this service efficiently, some Japanese tour wholesalers stock many *omiyage* items in their own warehouses in Japan and deliver them from there. For example, a honeymoon couple might order an Australian wine set (red and white wines) and have it delivered to the residence of their *nakoodo* the day after their scheduled return from Australia. The couple may arrange the same service for many relatives and friends and save a lot of precious honeymoon time. This service is also popular among busy Japanese executives who wish to spend as much time as possible on golf courses rather than on souvenir hunting.

One major tour wholesaler has started the *omiyage* telephone center, with business hours from 8:00 A.M. to midnight. Shoppers can look at the special gift catalog and call in their orders and pay by credit card. They can have the center arrange for airport pickup or the home delivery service, whichever is more convenient. Recently, this company also started the flower gift Japan home delivery service. This innovative gift service provides delivery of a variety of flower bouquets and potted plants from several foreign countries: vanda orchids from Thailand and Singapore; anthuriums, cattleyas, and proteas from Hawaii; carnations from California; tulips from Holland; baskets of kiwis from New Zealand; potted pineapple plants from the Philippines; and potted kangaroo paw plants from Australia.

Japanese visitors often use the services of Japanese freight forwarders that have branch offices at overseas tourist destinations. Many visitors, especially those who travel to several cities or countries, want to send souvenirs to Japan from each stop instead of carrying them around throughout the trip. Because they use *takkyuubin* (home delivery service) very frequently in Japan, they may also feel they should do the same while traveling abroad. This delivery service is an extremely convenient method of sending souvenirs, suitcases, golf bags, china, paintings, and other bulky items to Japan. Tour companies, department stores, specialty stores, and even individuals can arrange to have one of the home delivery service companies pick up a shipment and send it to Japan. Shipments are processed as follows: a customer hands over the shipment with a detailed description to a representative of a freight forwarder; he fills out an unaccompanied baggage declaration form and has it approved by a Japanese customs officer upon arrival in Japan; he sends the approved customs form to the freight forwarder office in Japan. In the meantime, staff members with the freight forwarder's overseas branch office prepare all the entry documents and send the shipment via air cargo service. When the shipment arrives in Japan and the stamped unaccompanied baggage form is received from the customer, the staff of its Japan office will clear customs and send the shipment to the customer's home. The customer will pay all freight and handling charges, duties, and taxes (if applicable) upon delivery in Japanese yen. One tax advantage for this method of shipment is that goods sent as unaccompanied baggage are considered personal effects. And these are included in the duty-free allowance of $2,000 and not subject to the regular import duties levied on commercial shipments.

Discount Stores

More economy-minded Japanese visitors now go to discount stores to hunt for bargains rather than to regular souvenir shops. They even go to flea markets to buy local handicrafts, inexpensive clothing, toys, and other items. What they buy at discount stores may or may not be suitable for *omiyage,* but they feel they can save a lot of money if they go to these stores. For example, ABC Discount Store Chains, with some forty outlets in the Waikiki area alone, do a brisk business with Japanese shoppers. Some Japanese visitors even shop at huge national warehouse distribution centers such as Price-Costco, Walmart, Sam's Club, and Kmart. These shoppers do not seem to mind the inconvenience of carrying bulky souvenir items themselves.

Effective Sales Approaches and Tactics

Merchants who do not understand cultural differences in sales approaches and sales talks may run into serious problems. Japanese shoppers expect to be treated courteously, just as they are in Japan. If they are not given the same prompt and courteous service, they may become frustrated and unhappy. The old cliché, "The customer is king," is taken seriously as the standard code of retail service in Japan. The traditional attitude of Japanese merchants has always been *okyaku-sama wa kamisama desu* (the customer is god). Salespersons must use polite language, a courteous sales approach, proper sales talk, and special sales tactics if they wish to be successful in selling to Japanese shoppers.

Social Status and Japanese Language

In Japan, customers are always considered to have higher status than salespeople. Customers pay for the merchandise, and their purchases bring benefits to the salespeople and the store. All Japanese salespeople are trained to be courteous and sensitive to shoppers' needs. Their training focuses on good customer service attitudes, proper bows, polite gestures, and use of polite language. They must also gain a good knowledge of all merchandise they are selling.

Japanese store managers always try to instill and maintain good customer service attitudes among their staff by holding a *choorei* (brief morning meeting) every morning before work begins. For example, each department of a large Japanese department store holds this meeting before the store opens. Department managers make short remarks on how employees should conduct themselves that day, and they challenge everyone to do their best in serving customers. When the store opens with the sound of chimes, all managers and salespeople line up along the main entrance hallway. As the first group of shoppers walk through, they all bow and say in chorus, *"Irasshaimase"* (welcome to our store), repeatedly. As soon as this greeting is over, all rush back to their respective departments and prepare to serve the first customer. They are not allowed to arrange merchandise after the store opens, as they are expected to be ready before the first customer approaches the sales counter. Perhaps this particular approach of starting the business day cannot be used by stores in Western countries, but it shows that instilling such an "attitude of gratitude" in the minds of salespeople is critical in serving Japanese customers.

Greetings are considered very important in Japanese culture. All new employees are given a series of drills on how to bow and greet properly. In fact, they cannot keep their jobs unless they actually master the art of proper greeting. They should be able to say all greetings in such a manner that will show a sincere attitude, politeness, willingness, and enthusiasm. All Japanese retailers say, "Every sale begins with a proper greeting."

Facial expressions, gestures, postures, and personal appearance are also important because Japanese shoppers understand and appreciate a friendly attitude shown through nonverbal behavior. Salespeople must learn to smile properly, make hand gestures politely, take a low posture, and maintain a neat and pleasant appearance. They should have a nice smile, but not a big grin. They should not point at a customer with the index finger. Instead, they should use a polite hand gesture, brief eye contact, or a shallow bow to get the attention of a certain customer. They must always be ready to bow and show appreciation. Male sales-people are expected to wear conservative business suits or store uniforms, neckties, neatly pressed white shirts, shined shoes, and have short hair, short fingernails, no beard, and no conspicuous jewelry. Female salespeople are usually required to wear store uni-forms. They are not allowed to have long hair, too much makeup, long fingernails with bright red nail polish, conspicuous jewelry, or other accessories that might offend customers.

It is also important for salespeople to learn polite expres-sions because Japanese is a status-oriented language. Japanese has many personal pronouns and several levels of politeness. One example is that the English personal pronoun "you" has eight dif-ferent forms (in order of politeness) in Japanese: *otaku-sama, soch-ira-sama, anata-sama, anata, an'ta, kimi, omae,* and *temee.* The last four pronouns are never used when addressing persons of supe-rior status. The pronoun *anata,* which is the direct translation of "you," is almost never used when addressing a customer. The most common way of addressing a customer is by using *okyaku-sama,* which literally means Mr./Mrs./Miss Customer. *Okyaku-sama* can be used whether the customer is young or old, male or female, married or single. (In some instances personal pronouns can be omitted in Japanese, as in Spanish.) A simple English expression, "Which one do you like?" can be translated into six different expressions as follows in order of politeness: *Dochira ga ousuki desu ka? Dochira ga suki desu ka? Dore ga suki desu ka? Dore ga suki ka? Docchi ga suki ka? Docchi?* These examples demonstrate how care-ful Japanese salespeople should be in choosing the most appropri-ate pronoun and expression for each situation. Obviously, an incorrect choice would be deemed disrespectful and could result in a lost sale. This also means that English-speaking salespeople should use polite expressions so as not to offend Japanese custom-ers. Many Japanese do not understand English very well, but they do understand how they are spoken to and treated by salespeople.

Courteous Sales Approaches

In the Western cultural context, salespeople usually try to elimi-nate any status barriers when they talk with prospective customers. In some instances, they may even ask customers for permission to use their first names. But in Japan a clear status distinction is maintained between salespeople and customers without exception. The customer's last name is always used with *sama* or *san,* such as Tanaka-sama or Tanaka-san.

Some American salespeople try to become too friendly with Japanese customers. They may even joke around by speaking broken Japanese or by speaking "childish" English, when they should be polite and sincere. This type of behavior is not only unacceptable but also very insulting to status-conscious Japanese customers. An overtly friendly approach will backfire on salespeople, although they may not mean to offend customers.

An aggressive and persistent approach is usually not effective. The Japanese are basically shy and unfriendly toward total strangers. When they walk into a retail store for the first time, they rarely respond to a salesperson's greeting. They may even avoid eye contact if they simply want to look around. Salespeople should not push customers too hard to buy something. Some Japanese shoppers come in just to size up a store first, and they may come back with others if they have a good impression of the store and the salespeople. They usually buy on the second visit, especially when they are buying expensive items. Obviously, first impressions are very important to Japanese customers.

Japanese shoppers prefer to do business with someone they know personally rather than any representative of the store who happens to be on duty. They often seek an introduction to a certain salesperson of the store from a former customer or tour company staff with whom they are acquainted. This is particularly true when they intend to buy expensive merchandise such as jewelry and watches. In Japan, all salespeople and even managers wear name tags so that customers can remember their names. They also hand out business cards and invite customers to ask for them on their next shopping visit. These practices are intended to personalize the customer-salesperson relationship and to promote the public image of the store as warm and friendly. Salespeople should also remember the names of former customers who make many referrals.

In contrast to the usually shy Japanese shoppers, there are some very aggressive shoppers who demand immediate attention. A certain group of Japanese business executives, for example, may behave impatiently and rudely toward a salesperson. As they are usually pampered in Japan, they often think they can demand the same service even in foreign countries. They may even show off a bundle of big bills in their hands. They will usually buy a lot of expensive merchandise as souvenirs if the salesperson can remain cool and treat them courteously.

Proper Sales Talk

Aggressive persuasion is considered important for effective sales in Western culture, particularly in the United States. American salespeople who are trained to never take no for an answer would be too aggressive and brash for Japanese shoppers. They also tend to talk too much and listen too little. In some instances, they may even try to push something that shoppers are not really interested in buying. Openly aggressive and insistent sales talk should be replaced with a polite and patient service-oriented sales talk.

Typical Japanese-style sales talk begins with a proper greeting and a show of gratitude, as mentioned earlier. *Irasshaimase* (welcome) and *maedo arigatoo gozaimasu* (thank you for your continued patronage) are the most common greetings used by Japanese salespeople. They must sound sincere and pleasant at the same time. The cheerful and active atmosphere created by the greetings is very important even before any sales talk begins. In fact, most smaller Japanese retail stores demand that the entire sales staff and the managers say *irasshaimase* in unison to all customers when they enter the store, and *arigatoo gozaimashita* (thank you for your patronage) when they leave, whether or not the customers have purchased anything.

It is always important to begin the first stage of the selling process by asking questions about customers' hometowns, travel experiences, weather, sports, and other pleasant topics. This is an effective way of establishing a rapport with them and making them feel comfortable. It might be a good idea to talk about sumo wrestling, baseball, or soccer. If a customer is referred by a tour company, the salesperson must recognize this referral and say something like, "That's a fine company. We always give special service to their tour members." Many young Japanese visitors come in with guidebook in hand and ask for specific items advertised in the book. In fact, they might have read several books and magazines that provide shopping guides before arrival at a destination. Naturally, they would be disappointed if they could not find the items they had planned to buy.

The second stage of the selling process is to find out what the customer is buying and why and what price range they have in mind. Many Japanese visitors buy one or two expensive souvenirs for themselves as a memento of their overseas trip. It could be a Cartier diamond ring, a Gucci handbag, a Rolex watch, or a Dunhill attaché case. All visitors buy a large number of souvenirs for their friends and relatives. The price range for each souvenir is determined by how much money has been received and for whom it is intended. They also buy things that their friends and relatives have asked them to buy. Some proper questions for salespeople to ask would be:

> *Kore wa gojibun de otsukaini narimasu ka?*
> (Are you going to use this yourself?)

> *Kore wa taisetsu na okyaku-sama e no omiyage desu ka?*
> (Is this gift for your important client?)

> *Otomodachi no okaimono desu ka?*
> (Are you buying these for your friends?)

> *Goyosan wa oikura gurai desu ka?*
> (About how much do you wish to spend?)

The third and final stage of the selling process is to help customers decide what to buy. The salesperson should not push certain items against their will, but should be patient and helpful in completing the planned purchases according to information obtained from the above sample questions. The salesperson should even take notes to avoid leaving out gifts for important clients and relatives and should act more like a shopping consultant rather than an aggressive salesperson with a "fat" commission check in mind. With Japanese shoppers, recommendations and suggestions seem to work better than aggressive persuasion and control.

Special Sales Tactics

There are certain sales tactics that have proved to be effective in selling to Japanese visitors. Discounts, gift-wrapping services, and a good after-service are just a few.

In Japan, it is common for tourist shops to give discounts to customers who buy several items at one time. And a *saabisuhin* (small gift) is usually given to preferred customers. It could be a small sample bottle of French perfume or a fifty-millimeter bottle of Hennessy cognac. Tourist shops always offer special discount prices to certain people. For example, a sales manager may give a substantial discount and special service to a good friend of a local tour company manager who sends a large number of visitors each year. The manager may also give discounts to new customers who are friends of regular customers. In this way, the manager honors *kao* (face) of those who refer new customers to the shop. Undoubtedly, people who refer friends will say something like, "If you go to ABC Store and mention my name, you will get a discount." And if the shopkeeper there does not honor that statement, the person who made this introduction will lose face and be embarrassed.

All tourist shops that want to have Japanese visitors as clientele should adopt a flexible pricing policy and be ready to give discounts to "special" customers. Some clever tourist shop owners in Hawaii do not charge Japanese customers Hawaii state tax and advertise that their shops are "duty free." They call it a "special" discount when in fact this tax is included in the sales price of all merchandise. Japanese customers often insist on receiving discounts by saying, for example, *"Kimochi dake waribikishite kudasai"* (please give me a small discount from your heart). Indeed, a small discount seems to make a big difference in completing a difficult sale to insistent Japanese customers.

At the same time, too much of a discount can defeat the very purpose of making a sale. If the price of a diamond ring is suddenly discounted by 50 percent at one time, Japanese shoppers will suspect that the salesperson is dishonest and untrustworthy. They will naturally become suspicious of any tourist shop that sells all of its merchandise at a 50 percent discount. If drastic discounting needs to be done, the salesperson must present a legitimate and believable excuse for it. Trust is the most important factor to any shoppers.

Gift-wrapping services are very important to Japanese shoppers. Since *teisai* (outward appearance) is highly valued, they like to have every purchase put into a box and wrapped neatly with a sheet of good quality wrapping paper. Sometimes the box and the wrapping of a gift from Japan look more expensive than the merchandise itself. If shoppers go to a famous department store, they may want to have their purchase gift-wrapped with paper bearing the store's logo. Evidently the Japanese wish to implicitly communicate that they bought the gift at a famous store. For non-Japanese store owners, providing good gift-wrapping services might seem wasteful and too time consuming, but it is an excellent method of promoting the store's image and its merchandise. Many Japanese shoppers are actually shocked to see that their purchases are nonchalantly thrown into plastic bags and handed to them. They also find it too cumbersome to go to the service center and wait in line for gift wrapping. If a gift-wrapping service is too troublesome for a store, it would be acceptable to give several sheets of wrapping paper, boxes, and shopping bags for customers to take home.

After-services are extremely critical in selling to Japanese visitors because they cannot easily return the merchandise they have purchased overseas. Stores that are successful in catering to them provide efficient and dependable after-service within Japan. For example, the most successful duty-free shop chains with many branches in the United States, Guam, Saipan, Australia, New Zealand, Hong Kong, Singapore, and Thailand have always maintained customer service centers in Tokyo and Osaka. These centers handle all complaints from Japanese customers who have mistakenly been given the wrong or damaged merchandise. The shops guarantee every purchase almost unconditionally and take quick action to solve any problem at their expense. Customers usually do not mind paying more for their purchases if they are assured good quality and dependable after-service in Japan.

Japanese tour companies never recommend shops that do not offer good after-service because they might be blamed for recommending irresponsible stores. If their clients are unhappy with the souvenir stores' merchandise, they are more likely to complain to the tour companies after they return to Japan, instead of filing complaints against the stores directly. The tour companies are morally responsible, even though they are not legally responsible for the souvenir shops' failings.

Handling money and receiving payment from Japanese shoppers can be an interesting experience. They usually carry a lot of cash (sometimes in a money belt tied around the waist). One reason they do this is that *senbetsu* are always in cash, and another reason is that cash is still used more often for shopping in Japan.

Souvenir shops should have currency conversion tables at each cash register for quick reference. The salesperson should be able to show Japanese shoppers the yen equivalent of their purchase when asked. When receiving Japanese yen for payment, the stores should not try to make extra money through currency exchanges. Many Japanese visitors know the daily exchange rate of yen and would be very upset if they had to exchange their money at an unreasonably high rate. Honesty will bring more business!

Explaining local taxes is also important because many Japanese who do not read English may think the added tax is an extra item they have not bought. They invariably count the items and the columns of figures and mistakenly think they have been overcharged. If salespeople are unable to explain, the shops should have a clear explanation in Japanese on a sheet of paper so that the shoppers can read and understand it. Misunderstandings over money handling should be avoided at all cost to ensure good customer relations with Japanese shoppers.

Chapter 8

Air Transportation and Local Sightseeing Tours

Dependable and frequent air transportation is the most critical element in developing the international visitor industry. With the tremendous advancements in air transport technology in the past few decades, international airlines now provide thousands of daily flights to many tourist destinations around the world. International travelers can reach any destination with ease in a matter of hours. Transfers and sightseeing tours are provided to international visitors in comfortable climate-controlled buses and limousines. When the visitors go to hot and humid tropical destinations, they are transferred in air-conditioned vehicles and taken to scenic spots. When they go to destinations where the outside temperature is too low to be comfortable, they travel in comfortably heated vehicles. While Japanese visitors really enjoy all of these physical comforts, they also expect good personalized service. As in other aspects of visitor services, their expectations are obviously different from other international visitors. Understanding their special expectations is key to successful marketing of both air transportation and sightseeing tour services.

Air Transportation and Passenger Service

Japanese visitors are blessed with the convenience of frequent flights from international airports located in seventeen different cities throughout Japan. In fact, there are about 50 carriers that provide some 545,000 seats on their scheduled flights on a weekly basis to hundreds of foreign destinations. And during peak travel periods there are many more seats available to and from the most popular destinations on extra sections and charter flights. For example, it is estimated that several airlines brought in more than 350,000 Japanese visitors to Hawaii during the summer months of 1994 alone, which is 30 percent more than the average seasonal arrival.

The major international airports in Japan are located in Narita, Osaka, Nagoya, Fukuoka, Haneda, Sendai, Niigata, and Sapporo. Narita (New Tokyo International Airport) is the busiest airport, served by 46 major international airlines providing 315,400 seats weekly, and Kansai International Airport is second busiest, served by 31 airlines providing 123,200 seats weekly. Nagoya is the third busiest airport, served by 22 airlines providing 44,000 seats weekly, Fukuoka is served by 17 airlines providing 30,000 seats, Haneda is served by one airline (China Airlines) providing 10,000 seats, Sendai is served by three airlines providing 4,800 seats, and Sapporo is served by five airlines providing 11,000 seats.[1] Keen competition among these international airlines for a bigger share of the ever-growing Japanese travel market not only provides higher frequency, but also promotes lower airfares. In addition, the airlines frequently offer promotional fares and huge discounts to certain foreign destinations in order to stimulate a new market segment. In some situations, airfares to foreign destinations are the same or even lower than airfares to domestic destinations.

It is becoming less expensive to fly nowadays. Airfares have dropped by an average of 2.6 percent per year from the 1960s to the early 1990s and are projected to continue to do so at a rate of 1 percent per year through 2010 due to the productivity improvements brought about by modern jet airplanes.[2] Lower airfares will undoubtedly stimulate more travel from Japan to foreign countries.

With this rapid increase in the number of flights, airlines need to devise efficient methods of handling large numbers of passengers. Although computerized reservation systems can expedite information storage and retrieval, reservations clerks still need to communicate with Japanese passengers either in Japanese or English. All Japanese airlines have enough English-Japanese bilingual reservation clerks to handle telephone calls. Many foreign airlines, however, have only a small number of bilingual clerks. They are compelled to make Japanese passengers wait for a long time before they can speak to one of their few Japanese-speaking reservation clerks. Sometimes callers have no choice but to listen to recorded messages in English that are played again and again. Since the Japanese are usually very impatient, they may just hang up in disgust and may fail to reconfirm their flights or notify the airlines of any changes they wish to make. If these Japanese passengers are traveling on FIT fares or "air only" on Group Inclusive Tour (GIT) fares, they cannot turn to a local Japanese tour operator for Japanese-language assistance. They usually book their own hotels and engage in independent recreational activities. In addition, more and more younger Japanese visitors will be traveling overseas, seeking fun and adventure on their own, although some cannot speak English very well.

One solution for minimizing the communication problem with Japanese-speaking passengers is to assign Japanese-speaking reservation clerks to designated phone numbers at all times and have them handle all calls in Japanese. Another solution may be to have all reservation clerks learn several commonly used words and phrases in Japanese, or have them practice speaking slowly and clearly (but not condescendingly) in English with those passengers who wish to speak in English. It should be remembered that English spoken over the telephone is more difficult to understand even for those people who can understand English fairly well in face-to-face situations.

At this time, there are no serious problems in communication at airport check-ins because the majority of Japanese passengers still travel in groups and are handled by a Japanese-speaking representative of their local tour operator. This situation is expected to change in the near future with the projected increase of Japanese passengers who travel independently of group tours and those who fly to foreign destinations that many Japanese have never been to. This trend apparently means that all passenger traffic agents will need to know enough Japanese to handle Japanese-speaking passengers. One stopgap measure currently taken by several airlines is to have a Japan group tour counter at the airport and assign a few Japanese-speaking agents to handle all Japanese-speaking passengers. However, this measure works only when the majority of Japanese passengers are checking in as groups. It will not work in the future when passengers start checking in as individuals.

The major complaint regarding passenger handling is that the traffic agents have become very impersonal and mechanical in their handling of passengers. They rarely make eye contact with passengers who are checking in. Instead, they tend to look at the computer screen. They often blurt out questions rapidly and try to finish the check-in procedure as soon as they can. They may sometimes ignore passengers' questions if they think the questions are insignificant or bothersome. Some airline critics say that today passenger handling is like cattle herding and is not the courteous service that major international airlines were once proud of. This type of poor service is also due to the recent cost-cutting measure of subcontracting check-ins to other airlines. Some smaller airlines do not have their own check-in counters. They have larger local airlines handle check-ins, baggage loading and unloading, aircraft cleaning, and even maintenance.

Handling delays and missed connections are other serious problems. Japanese passengers who cannot speak English will naturally be more worried and frustrated than English-speaking passengers. They can neither understand English announcements regarding revised flight schedules nor understand explanations as to why they missed their flight or what flight they are asked to take later. Passengers on business trips may feel especially inconvenienced and may demand immediate attention to their problems. In many situations, Japanese passengers may not receive the attention they deserve simply because they cannot speak good English. Japanese-speaking passenger service agents must see to it that these inconvenienced passengers are taken care of immediately.

Careless and arbitrary seat assignments can cause serious inconveniences for Japanese passengers. They always want to be seated with friends and family members because they are not sociable the way Westerners are. They may even hesitate to strike up conversations with fellow Japanese passengers if they are total strangers. Depending on the seating configuration of an aircraft, there are situations where even honeymoon couples are seated separately. Sometimes, the traffic agent may unintentionally assign Mr. and Mrs. So and So to different rows because newly married women are typically listed under their maiden names (passport names), not their spouses' surnames. The agent in charge should be aware of this fact and pay special attention to the newlyweds. Elderly passengers should be given isle seats near toilets and flight attendants' stations.

In-Flight Service

All international airlines advertise their superb in-flight service provided by attractive flight attendants in uniforms. Although fairly good service is still provided for first class passengers, in-flight service has generally deteriorated to a monotonous routine with poor meals for economy class passengers. Mass travel in jumbo jets has made international flights like a train or bus ride for all passengers, with the passengers herded in and out of the aircraft methodically. Overseas flights are no longer the "romantic fanfare" of a few decades ago.

Japanese passengers are rather particular as to the kinds of service provided by flight attendants. They expect the attendants to speak Japanese and to respond to their needs without delay. Although non-Japanese airlines hire Japanese-speaking flight attendants, they are often overworked because the ratio of these flight attendants to the number of Japanese passengers on board is uneven. For example, only four of fifteen flight attendants might be Japanese-speaking on a flight where 98 percent of the passengers are Japanese. This imbalance should be corrected by requiring all flight attendants to acquire at least the minimum level of competency in Japanese.

The *oshibori* (hot or cold hand towel) service and Japanese food service initially started by Japan Airlines have become available on non-Japanese airlines. Even American carriers flying trans-Pacific routes now offer sushi as hors d'oeuvres and *makunouchi bento* (deluxe box lunch) for dinner in first class and business class sections. And a small portion of Japanese foods are also included in economy class meals as well. Today, in-flight announcements are in both English and Japanese, as are flight magazines and video and audio programs. These accommodations for Japanese passengers undoubtedly pay a big dividend to many airlines. But it must be emphasized here again that efficient and courteous personalized service is the most important ingredient in satisfying all of the Japanese passengers' needs.

Transfer and Sightseeing Tours

Today large air-conditioned buses are used to transfer Japanese visitors on group tours, and the same buses are used for sightseeing tours. Japanese groups prefer traveling in their own chartered bus to joining another group on the same bus, even when the groups are not large enough to fill all the seats. This preference comes from their habit of traveling in a privately chartered bus in Japan. They usually stock up on drinks and food and start merrymaking when they get on board for the several hour drive to a hot-spring resort. Nowadays, there is a special type of sightseeing bus called a "saloon bus," which has comfortable swivel seats, a *karaoke* machine, a few microphones, and a refrigerator stocked with beer, whiskey, soft drinks, and snacks. The accompanying bus guide giving tour narrations acts as emcee for the *karaoke* contest and also sings a few folk songs to entertain the passengers.

Japanese tour wholesalers do not want to mix customers who are on different types of package tours. They are afraid that the passengers may talk to each other about the tour prices they have paid before departure. For example, a person who has paid fifteen hundred dollars for a deluxe package tour should not be riding the same bus with someone who has paid only eight hundred dollars for a similar tour to the same destination. Consequently, more buses may be required to accommodate different groups of Japanese visitors.

For super deluxe tours, Japanese tour operators use Cadillac, Lincoln, or Mercedes Benz limousines to give tour members more privacy. For example, for a deluxe honeymoon tour, a large limousine will be used for just one couple. For smaller groups tour operators use mini buses so that each group can travel separately. Even though there is an old saying, *Tabi wa michizure* (A good traveling companion met on a trip makes the trip more enjoyable), the Japanese are not as sociable and open as they could be when traveling abroad.

Taxi service in some countries is confusing to Japanese visitors. In Japan, there are two ways to get a taxi. The first is to go to a taxi stand by a hotel, train station, or large shopping center. Another way is to flag down a taxi passing by on the street. (A Japanese taxi has a big illuminated sign on the dash board that says,

"Empty," "Hired," or "Not in Service.") This is the reason why some Japanese visitors try to flag a taxi in a foreign city where passenger pickup on the street is not allowed. They may also expect the taxi door to open and close automatically, as all Japanese taxis have an automatic door. Their expectations sometimes anger foreign taxi drivers because they may wait for the door to open and not bother to close it when they get out. Finally, tipping is not done in Japan except in rare cases, and this also angers taxi drivers who expect tips from all passengers.

With regard to sightseeing tours, Japanese visitors expect licensed professional tour guides to provide tour narrations. In Japan, all tour guides for foreign visitors are certified by the Japanese Ministry of Transport. They must not only acquire professional-level competency in foreign languages, but must also pass rigorous tests on Japanese politics, history, economy, cultural anthropology, botany, and other related subjects of interest. They are also required to have commonsense knowledge of the home country of the visitors with whom they come in contact. They should be able to make frequent references and comparisons to the visitors' countries when they speak about Japan. For example, a licensed English-speaking guide should have ample knowledge about the United States, Canada, England, Australia, and New Zealand. Unfortunately, tour guides in many foreign countries are neither fully licensed nor adequately trained. As a result, many Japanese visitors complain that the tour narrations are inaccurate and different from what they have read in travel books and tourist magazines. In Australia, New Zealand, and Canada, tour companies are forced to hire as tour guides young Japanese office clerks or students who are on a one-year working holiday visa. While these young people can speak good Japanese, they may not have enough knowledge of the country they are talking about because they are visitors themselves. Any country catering to Japanese visitors must train native-born tour guides to become "unofficial ambassadors" representing their own country. Ideally, all tour guides should be individuals who were born, raised, and educated in the country in which they work as guides and narrators. There is no substitute for the firsthand knowledge and actual experiences acquired by living in one's own country for many years.

Chapter 9

Nonverbal Communication in Customer Contacts

People generally believe that if they cannot communicate with Japanese visitors they should use nonverbal means of communication. This belief is based on the common assumption that nonverbal behavior is the same or at least very similar across cultures. But this assumption is not totally accurate. Such common nonverbal behaviors as facial expressions, eye contact, gestures, body movements, posture, physical appearance, use of personal space, touching, and time usage are interpreted differently from culture to culture. Misinterpretation of these nonverbal expressions will cause serious misunderstandings and unexpected problems. Japanese nonverbal behavior is no exception. Therefore, hotel and restaurant workers, souvenir shop salespeople, transportation company workers, and others who come in direct contact with Japanese customers should know exactly what each nonverbal behavior means in various situations.

Facial Expressions

In Hollywood movies, so-called expressionless faces and sinister smiles are associated with the images of Japanese men. These images may be quite funny and entertaining to Westerners, but they also show that some Japanese facial expressions are indeed confusing and difficult for them to understand. Unlike friendly Americans, the Japanese do not smile at strangers or spontaneously strike up a conversation. They usually wear a "public" face that is rather impassive and nearly devoid of expression because controlling one's emotions in public is a virtue in Japan. Uninhibited emotional expression is tolerated only in very young children and among one's closest friends or relatives.

Laughing and smiling are generally considered signs of happiness, joy, or agreement in most Western cultures, but the Japanese may also smile and laugh when expressing emotions such as embarrassment, anger, confusion, or sadness, or when apologizing. The following examples illustrate this difference: (1) A Japanese hotel guest may smile when he or she cannot understand what the front desk clerk is explaining in English. This smile actually means, "I don't really understand what you are saying, but I am too embarrassed to say that I don't understand you"; (2) A Japanese restaurant customer laughingly scolds the waitress who has brought a wrong dish after a long delay. This laugh means, "I am so upset with you, but I am merely hiding my anger in front of others. Bring me the correct dish immediately"; (3) A middle-aged Japanese man smilingly apologizes to a police officer, explaining that he has lost his wallet to a pickpocket. This smile does not mean that he is careless about his lost wallet, but rather, "It is so stupid of me to lose my wallet. I am so ashamed of myself!"; (4) A Japanese customer who has smashed a rental car in a traffic accident laughingly talks to the car rental company representative about it. This laugh means, "I am so embarrassed! How could this happen to me!"

However, not all Japanese smiles and laughter are ambiguous and used to conceal obvious emotions. There are happy smiles and laughter. The following are the five common types of laughter used by different people: (1) "Big" laughter, which is usually reserved for men only. This laughter is often heard when they respond to funny stories while having a good time; (2) Snickering or cackling. People often use this laughter when they are poking fun at someone else; (3) Concealed laughter, which is not loud. It is usually used when persons of inferior status want to laugh at those of higher status; (4) Embarrassed laughter, which is used when someone is embarrassed by his or her own stupid actions; (5) Flattering laughter, which is used to compliment someone on an outstanding accomplishment. It is not sincere but is socially appropriate; (6) Social laughter, which is usually used by socialites who want to impress those around them.[1] Japanese women often cover their mouths when they laugh or smile. This is considered a mark of femininity, especially among young high-society women. According to the old Japanese social etiquette, "cultured" women are not supposed to show their teeth when they laugh or smile.

Eye Contact

Eye contact is quite important in face-to-face situations because everyone uses their eyes to express different moods or feelings such as joy, happiness, sincerity, anger, surprise, disappointment, or fear. However, there is an obvious culture clash in interpreting eye contact used by the Japanese. In the American cultural context, sustained eye contact usually indicates that people are interested, honest, sincere, or happy. Avoidance of eye contact or a shifting of the eyes means that they are disinterested, dishonest, or sly. In Japanese culture, the same sustained eye contact means aggression, rudeness, insistence of equality, or belligerence. For example, an American mother may scold her disobedient son by saying, "Johnny, look at Mommy! I am talking to you!" And if he casts his eyes down, she will say, "You are lying to me again!" On the other hand, if a Japanese boy were to look directly at his mother's eyes while she was scolding him, she might say, "Why are you staring at me like that? You aren't afraid of me, are you? I'll tell your father. You have no respect for me!"

Because of this apparent difference in early childhood acculturation, Japanese visitors may misunderstand the meanings of proper eye contact. An American hotel manager would be considered rude and overbearing if he or she, to show respect, maintained eye contact with the Japanese guest whose room was burglarized. The manager is expected to have downcast eyes and apologize to the guest by bowing very low. In another context, sustained eye contact and a good smile by a young woman is often misinterpreted by Japanese men as personal interest. Young Japanese women almost never smile at male strangers, even when their eyes meet accidentally, unless they have a "hidden" intention.

This does not mean, however, that the Japanese never expect any eye contact. In fact, many Japanese visitors complain that retail store salespeople, hotel front desk clerks, and restaurant cashiers have no eye contact at all, but rather look at the computer screens in front of them. In fact, brief and frequent eye contact acknowledging their presence and a friendly smile are very important in serving Japanese customers.

Gestures

Using hand gestures is the most common method of communicating without words. However, many Japanese gestures have different meanings. There are polite gestures and impolite ones, and some should never be used. The following gestures are important to remember:

(a) "Me"
Pointing at the nose with the index finger. (The comparable American gesture is touching the upper chest with the index finger or the palm of the hand.)

(b) "You"
Pointing with the index finger is a common gesture, but this is not a gesture to use with a person of superior status. A polite gesture is to point with the whole hand with palm up as if offering something.

(c) "Come here"
Beckoning with open hand up and down with palm facing outward. This gesture is often misunderstood as "goodbye" by Americans. The same American gesture is to flap the fingers of the open hand inward. Neither of these beckoning gestures should be used to call a VIP

customer. A proper gesture is to make brief eye contact, a shallow bow, and pull the open hand (palm up) sideways.

(d) "No, I don't understand you" or "No, thank you."

Moving the open right hand back and forth as if fanning oneself or batting an insect from one's face. This gesture may mean "smelly" to Americans.

(e) "I am puzzled."

Scratching or stroking the back of the head.

(f) "I want to drink" or "Where is the bar?"

Holding up the cupped right hand, and moving it to the mouth as if drinking from it.

(g) "To eat" or "Where is the restaurant?"

Cupping the left hand near the mouth as if holding a bowl of rice, and going through the motion of using chopsticks with the index and middle fingers held together.

(h) "I want to smoke" or "Where can I buy cigarettes?"

Moving the right index and middle fingers back and forth toward the mouth.

(i) "Girlfriend" or "Wife"

Showing the little finger of the right hand pointed straight up. (An "adventurous" Japanese man might point at his nose with the index finger and make this gesture to a young woman. He means, "Would you like to be my girlfriend?")

(j) "Boss," "Manager," or "Husband"

Showing the thumb of the right hand straight up. This gesture does not mean "A-OK," as it does in the United States and in other Western countries. It is often used when the person wishes to say, "The boss is coming. Let's go back to work," or "Where is the manager? I want to talk to him," or "Is this your husband?"

(k) "Money"

Showing a circle formed by the index finger and the thumb, palm inward. An American "OK" gesture is similar, but it shows palm outward.

(l) "Close my account and give me the check."

Crossing the index fingers as if making an "X" mark.

(m) "No," "Not Open," or "Not permitted."

Crossing the hands in front of the body. (A late-evening shopper may use this gesture to ask, "Are you closed?")

Body Posture and Movements

Constant bowing can be the most confusing of all Japanese non-verbal behaviors. Westerners are often perplexed as to how to greet Japanese visitors properly. They must ask themselves whether they should shake hands or bow. In most instances it is not necessary for Westerners to learn and practice Japanese-style bows because Japanese visitors generally accept Western-style handshakes. But it is important to recognize that the Japanese consider *teishisei* (low posture) and bowing very desirable when greeting persons of higher social status. Naturally, the seemingly arrogant American cowboy style of standing tall and shaking hands would not be appropriate. Shaking hands with a slight bow would be more acceptable to the Japanese in almost all situations.

Bowing is certainly status oriented, and the relative status of each person in face-to-face interactions decides who initiates and stops bowing and who bows lower and longer. In fact, bowing is so ingrained in the Japanese that many of them automatically and unconsciously bow to each other even when they are talking on the phone. There are many books and training programs on proper bowing behavior. Japanese men, women, and children must learn several kinds of bows. It is important to know that men and women bow differently. Men bow with their hands on the side of the thighs, while women do so with their hands crossed in the front. The following are several situations illustrating proper bowing:

(a) A hotel assistant manager bowing to a VIP guest.

(b) A young child bowing to her uncle.

(c) A high school student bowing to her teacher.

(d) A salesperson bowing to an important customer.

(e) A hotel maid greeting a guest at a Japanese inn.

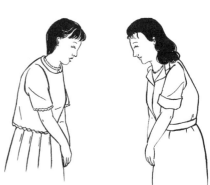

(f) Women of equal status bowing to each other.

Sitting Posture

One important bit of advice to Westerners, particularly American businesspeople, regarding proper sitting posture is that they should not cross their legs either at the knee or ankle when they talk to Japanese visitors. It is considered most disturbing for them to see female managers cross their legs at the knee when they are wearing skirts. They should have both feet on the floor, knees together, with arms on the lap. Having the ankle on the knee of the other leg is an extremely insulting posture even among good friends.

Physical Appearance

Japanese visitors are generally shorter and do not wear well-coordinated Western clothes, especially when they go to resort hotels. Some of them might even give Westerners the impression that they are "not wealthy enough" to receive courteous service. Certain groups of host nationals may resent Japanese who behave like "rich people" because they were not rich at all until a few decades ago.

Some Japanese guests may ignore dress codes in restaurants and hotels. They may enter a fine dining restaurant in a resort hotel wearing T-shirt, shorts, and rubber slippers. They may also walk around in the hotel lobby in swim shorts or bikinis. On the other hand, there are other Japanese guests who may overdress to show off expensive brand name clothing. Some men wear everything made by Dunhill, and some women wear everything made by Christian Dior. These people are using brand name items as "object language" to communicate that they are very rich people who deserve first-class service and courtesy. At any rate, discriminating against Japanese visitors based on their physical appearance alone would be very detrimental to customer relations.

Personal Space

Every culture defines the appropriate interpersonal distance for a variety of social situations. Every individual has his or her own personal space, which is an invisible demarcation. He or she may feel uncomfortable or threatened when this space is invaded, intentionally or unintentionally. It appears that the Japanese do not mind living and working in overcrowded urban centers, but they are "noncontact" people who cannot tolerate close personal proximity. Bowing distance is wider than handshaking distance. In public places such as trains, subways, busy streets, restaurants, and shops, they are quite adept in using defense mechanisms to protect themselves from invasions into their personal boundaries. They change their posture, hold their arms in front, or avoid eye contact. For example, Japanese men do not face each other directly, but stand or sit side by side. They may intentionally fail to recognize others' presence by totally ignoring them. Generally speaking, Japanese people rarely say, "Excuse me" when they bump into others accidentally. They are polite to one another among coworkers, friends, and relatives, but they can be very impolite and cold toward total strangers.

Touching and Kissing

Japanese mothers tend to have frequent and intimate body contact with their infants, and they sleep in the same room with them until the children are one or two years old. But as they grow older, the children will have less and less bodily contact with their mothers. Japanese husbands and wives hesitate to hold hands and walk around unless they are honeymooners or full-mooners traveling overseas. Consequently, it is not considered polite to hold hands, hug shoulders, or embrace Japanese visitors. The social kissing practiced in the United States and in Latin American countries is very embarrassing to many Japanese unless they have lived overseas and learned to accept this type of greeting. The Hawaiian-style lei greeting with a kiss on the visitor's cheek is amusing and embarrassing to some Japanese visitors to Hawaii.

When shaking hands, Japanese businessmen may hold the hands of the other person a little too long. This awkward behavior perhaps comes from the custom of bowing several times while they exchange greetings. They often shake hands and bow at the same time. They may also avert their eyes when shaking hands because they feel that direct eye contact is overbearing and too aggressive. Young girls hold hands and walk around in Japan without being accused of having homosexual tendencies. It is socially acceptable for good friends, sisters, and schoolmates to hold hands and show friendship. (This particular behavior is acceptable only among elderly women in the United States.) In Japan, it is quite common for young women to go to discos and dance with other female friends, but kissing is a social taboo under normal circumstances.

Time Usage

Time is another important variable of nonverbal language, as how time is used can communicate different meanings. In Japanese culture, punctuality communicates respect and efficiency, and tardiness means disrespect and inefficiency. Trains, factory production lines, and offices run on clock time like any other industrialized nation, but Japan's "cultural clock" does not run in the same way. The Japanese use time in a "polychronic" (doing multiple things at a time) manner, whereas American use it in the "monochronic" (doing one thing at a time) manner. For example, a tourist shop salesperson may ring up a sale for one customer and, at the same time, answer a question from another customer. This is one of the reasons why Japanese shoppers gather around the cash register and ask for attention simultaneously.

All stores and restaurants in Japan have specific business hours posted clearly, but these business hours are quite flexible and extended almost at will. In other words, the businesses run on "customer-oriented time" in Japan, not on "clock-oriented time" as in Western countries. In fact, stores and restaurants are open as long as customers are there, even though official business hours may be over. Many Japanese shoppers are annoyed by department store announcements that they will close in fifteen minutes and by being rushed by sales clerks when they are still shopping. Customers expect the store to be kept open either by sales supervisors or managers until the last customer is properly served. They would never accept a statement such as, "We are closed. Please come back again tomorrow."

This time concept clearly reflects the vertical nature of Japanese society where high-status persons (buyers) can demand more time and immediate attention from low-status persons (sellers). Impatient Japanese customers may walk out if they are not given prompt and efficient service. Adjectives or adverbs describing informal time are quite vague and confusing. For example, in Western culture "right away," "shortly," and "a little while" can be five minutes, thirty minutes, or even half a day, depending on the situation. To busy Japanese shoppers or restaurant customers, "right away" literally means only a few minutes. Indeed, it is very important to understand how Japanese visitors perceive proper time usage and to make an effort to accommodate their demands on quick service.

PART III

DOING BUSINESS WITH

JAPANESE TRAVEL COMPANIES

The structure of the Japanese travel industry is very unique in that it is controlled by a handful of major travel companies. Many of these companies are members of large business conglomerates, and they have many subsidiaries in travel-related businesses. All of the major companies belong to the Japan Association of Travel Agents (JATA). They operate the travel business in accordance with rather rigid governmental rules and regulations. Obtaining a business license from the Japanese government for tour wholesaling and retailing requires a large sum of capital investment. The government also requires that managers of travel agencies be certified as travel consultants.

Establishing new business relations with Japanese tour companies can be a frustrating experience for foreign businessmen. Japanese tour company managers and representatives speak fairly good English and appear to be Westernized, but they usually conduct business in a way that is uniquely Japanese. They are difficult to approach without proper introductions, and they do not negotiate business contracts based on common Western business customs and practices. They make decisions by using different means and for different reasons. They like to solve business disputes in a cordial manner rather than through litigations. They prefer to maintain good business relations through constant face-to-face communication, instead of communicating by letter, telephone, and facsimile message. Those who want to do business with Japanese tour companies must understand the unique structure of the Japanese travel industry and study the culturally acceptable ways of doing business with Japanese businessmen in this industry.

Chapter 10

Japanese Travel Agencies and Tour Products

There are a total of 12,003 travel agencies on Japan, 848 of which are General Travel Agencies, 6,792 are Domestic Travel Agencies, and 4,363 subagencies.[1] As in other Japanese industries, the Japanese travel agency industry has a hierarchical structure primarily based on the financial strength of respective travel companies and their major stockholders. Most of these companies are not public corporations. They are either partially or wholly owned subsidiaries of major railways, airlines, shipping lines, large hotel chains, giant life and casualty insurance companies, and leading financial institutions. Many others are in-house travel agencies of large business conglomerates. Consequently, the distribution networks of travel products in Japan are dominated by major tour wholesalers and a small number of large travel agencies. In fact, more than 80 percent of the total travel business is controlled by the General Travel Agencies while slightly less than 20 percent is controlled by the Domestic Travel Agencies. The four largest travel agencies, namely Japan Travel Bureau (JTB), Kinki Nippon Tourist (KNT), Nippon Travel Agency (NTA), and Tokyu Tourist Corporation[2] control 35.3 percent of the travel market; another group of 31 larger travel agencies control 21.1 percent; the next 35 large agencies control 55.8 percent; and all others share 19.8 percent of the market.[3] In the overseas travel market, this dominance by top agencies is even more evident. Total sales of the past several years show that JTB controlled 25 percent of the market, KNT controlled 13 percent, NTA controlled 9 percent, and Tokyu Tourist Corporation controlled 5 percent. Such uneven market shares reflect the hierarchical structure of the Japanese travel agency industry; the laws related to the travel industry imposed by Japan's

Ministry of Transport; the regulations administered by Japan Association of Travel Agencies (JATA), and the convenience, service, and block-booking discounts that can be provided only by these travel agencies.

JTB, originally established in 1912 as the Japan National Railway System's sales arm, is the largest travel company in Japan. Until the early 1960s it had been the only public corporation licensed by the Ministry of Transport to engage in both outbound and inbound international travel business. It was privatized in 1968. Even today, its major stockholders are JR (formerly Japan National Railways), the Japan Travel Bureau Foundation, and several major banks. Likewise, KNT is one of the subsidiaries of Kinki Nippon Railway Company, the largest railway system in the Kansai region, which owns several department stores and a professional baseball team. KNT's major stockholders are Kinki Nippon Railways, Kyoto Miyako Hotel, Kinki Express, Nihon Life Insurance, and Hakone Hotel and Tourist Service. NTA is owned by Nishi Nihon JR (West Japan Passenger Railways), Higashi Nihon JR (East Japan Passenger Railways), and Daiichi Kangyo Bank, Japan's largest bank. Tokyu Tourist Corporation is a subsidiary of the Tokyu Group, one of Japan's largest business conglomerates. Its major stockholders are Tokyu Express Railways, Nihon Life Insurance, Asahi Bank, Tokyu Real Estate Company, Tokyo Marine Insurance, Mitsui Shintaku Bank, and Sumitomo Life Insurance. Hankyu Express International is owned solely by the Hankyu Electric Railway Company, another major railway system in the Osaka area.[4]

Many other Japanese travel companies are subsidiaries of large corporations. Jalpak Company Ltd. is a subsidiary of Japan Airlines, and the All Nippon Airways World Tours Company is a wholly owned subsidiary of All Nippon Airways. The Yusen Air & Sea Service Company is a subsidiary of Nippon Yusen, one of Japan's largest shipping lines, and Mitsui Air & Sea Service Company is also the subsidiary of Mitsui Shipping Company. Nomura Securities Company, the largest stock brokerage company in Japan, owns Nomura Tourist Bureau, Hitachi Group owns Hitachi Travel Bureau; Toshiba Group owns Toshiba Tourist Corporation; and even Japan's Farmers Cooperatives own Co-Op Travel Service.

Government Control

The Ministry of Transport and prefectural governments control the travel agencies by imposing strict licensing laws on travel agency operations. A General Travel Agency (Ippan Ryokoo Gyoosha) licensed by the Ministry of Transport is permitted to organize and sell package tours for both domestic and international travel destinations. The agency is required to post a Business Guarantee Bond (Eigyoo Hoshookin) of ¥70 million and ¥7 million for each of its major offices. A Domestic Travel Agency (Kokunai Ryokoo Gyoosha) must register with the governor's office of the prefecture in which it operates. In addition, a General Travel Agency must post the Compensation Security Bonds (Bensai gyoomu Hoshookin) of ¥11.2 million and ¥1.4 million for each of its major retail outlets. The Domestic Travel Agency is permitted to engage in domestic travel business only, including organizing and selling package tours to domestic tourist destinations. Any Domestic Travel Agency, however, is permitted to engage in international travel programs, if it becomes a subagent of any General Travel Agency. Subagents of both General Travel Agencies and Domestic Travel Agencies are also permitted to engage in the international travel business on behalf of their parent agencies on a commission basis, if they can enter into a subagency contract with them. Because it is prohibitively expensive to post a large sum of money for the business guarantee bond and to qualify as a General Travel Agency, small independent travel companies are forced to operate as subagencies of several General Travel Agencies.

Another governmental control is that every branch of a General Travel Agency and its subagency offices must be staffed with at least one certified travel consultant *(ryokoo gyoomu toriatsukai shunin)*. To qualify for this designation, an applicant must have at least two years of on-the-job experience and take the required course work administered by JATA. Upon completion of this course, the applicant must pass a rigorous national examination to be certified as travel consultant. The courses cover a wide range of subjects considered important in handling travel arrangements and meeting all other needs of travelers. To qualify to become a certified travel consultant, the applicant must have good knowledge of the travel business and a proper attitude as tour escort;

basic knowledge of group tours, departures, transportation, overseas stays, return transportation, and arrival procedures; basic understanding of important laws and regulations on travel, air transportation, hotel accommodations, and other related matters; general knowledge of politics, culture, geography, social customs and travel-related topics of major destination countries; immigration laws and procedures (entry and exit) of Japan and of major foreign countries; passport application procedures, customs clearance, quarantine, and foreign exchange regulations; practical English language skills of speaking, listening, and writing in travel-related situations; efficient handling of travel accidents (fire, illness, theft, and so on) as tour escort.

Japan Association of Travel Agents Regulations

JATA is the only trade organization of travel agents in Japan. The association has about 890 regular members that are General Travel Agencies and some 2,357 associate members that are subagencies. This organization is commissioned by the Ministry of Transport to engage in a number of important activities for the entire travel industry. Its major functions are to improve services to travelers, handle complaints and settle claims from clients, promote professionalism by educating its members, and offer educational programs for the national examination of certified travel consultant designation. It also engages in research studies, publication of various information, and the conducting of public relations for its members. JATA is affiliated with such international travel organizations as the Universal Federation of Travel Agents' Associations (UFTAA), American Society of Travel Agents (ASTA), Pacific Area Travel Association (PATA), and World Tourism Organization (WTO).

Good membership standing in JATA is extremely important for any travel company doing business in Japan. Every member company and its employees must uphold a high ethical standard and conduct business in a proper professional manner. Any serious violation of JATA regulations would undermine the credibility of the company and would result in fines and possible expulsion.

Tour Wholesalers and Customer Service

Unlike more individualistic and independent Western travelers, almost all Japanese travelers depend on travel agencies for their travel arrangements. In fact, more than 91.1 percent of the Japanese use travel agencies for booking of their overseas trips, of which more than 78.9 percent of them buy package tours marketed by tour wholesalers.[5] There are a number of reasons why Japanese travelers choose to use travel agencies. The most frequently cited reasons are "availability of good package tours," "used that agency before," "told by employer to use that agency," "reliability," "recommended by friends and acquaintances," "kind customer service attitude," "convenient location," "well known," "good service," and "frequent advertising."[6]

Availability of good package tours is the key to success in marketing travel products for every major tour wholesaler. Each major tour wholesaler in Japan organizes and markets a variety of package tours to hundreds of overseas tourist destinations. These companies compete with each other by conducting research, planning, and organizing many different package tours by market segments, and by marketing them through an extensive network of retail outlets. All of these companies have their own research departments through which they constantly monitor economic forecasts and consumer trends and conduct surveys to get an indication of customer satisfaction. They frequently improve existing package tours and introduce new tours based on the most recent research findings. They spend huge sums of money to print and distribute millions of tour catalogs that include beautiful pictures in full color on good quality glossy paper. For example, JTB publishes semiannually one million or more copies of tour catalogs for all eight major regional markets: Tokyo, Osaka, Nagoya, Fukuoka, Sapporo, Sendai, Niigata, and Hiroshima. Each tour catalog on a specific destination has between 60 to 130 pages with many beautiful color photographs of scenery, hotels, restaurants, shops, visitor attractions, and many optional tour activities. In addition, JTB prints specialized tour pamphlets for honeymooners, fullmooners, golfers, students, and marathoners, and separate special sales campaign pamphlets to promote new destinations. JTB has one package tour brand name, "Look," for both deluxe and economy package tours. The tour catalogs of Look Tours are distributed through its nationwide network of 336 branches, 414 subagencies, and 6,819 affiliated agencies.

Jalpak likewise publishes tens of thousands of tour catalogs for its first brand named "I'LL" and second brand named "AVA," and distributes them through its 5 sales offices, 541 subagents, and 7,080 retail outlets throughout Japan. Unlike other tour wholesalers, this company concentrates on wholesaling its package tours through the nationwide network of its affiliate retail travel agencies. It is a subsidiary of Japan Airlines and should not, in theory, compete directly against other tour wholesalers that use Japan Airlines' services. However, Japan Airlines has another subsidiary called Japan Tours Systems (JTS) that engages in both domestic and international travel businesses through its nationwide retail networks.

Availability of a wide variety of package tours is not the only convenience provided by travel agencies. Almost all retail travel agencies are "one-stop travel shops" that provide every possible convenience for their clients. Overseas travelers can request that their travel agency obtain passports, visas (or tourist cards), and other travel documents on their behalf. They can buy travelers' checks, travel insurance, optional tours, and prearrange shipment of *omiyage* from the places they plan to visit even before their departure. Young Japanese travelers who wish to combine their wedding and honeymoon at a foreign destination can have the tour wholesaler arrange everything for them.

The convenient services provided by Japanese tour wholesalers do not end in Japan. All of the major Japanese tour wholesalers have their own ground tour operators in almost all key tourist destinations around the world. All of these overseas subsidiaries have additional branch offices in other city locations and travel desks in major hotels. These overseas offices cater to clients who have purchased package tours from them. JTB Group currently employs more than 10,000 people at 385 offices in Japan and at 62 overseas branch offices. It also has 127 subsidiary companies that engage in travel business and many other businesses such as retail merchandising, hotel operations, real estate development, publishing, travel-related education and even health care.[7]

Jalpak has its own overseas service networks of 60 companies with offices at 100 locations. These overseas subsidiaries of Jalpak employ more than 1,500 people.[8] Jalpak provides travel desk services at major hotels and at hotels owned and/or managed by JAL Hotel System, another subsidiary of Japan Airlines. In addition, Jalpak has other subsidiaries and subcontractors that provide bus transportation, deluxe limousine services, golf tours, wedding services, and souvenirs. Evidently, these services are very convenient and invaluable to Japanese travelers who visit foreign countries. Recently, the overseas subsidiaries of major Japanese tour wholesalers have begun an outbound travel section that takes care of airline reservations and ticketing, hotel reservations, car rental reservations, and the travel needs of their local clients.

Bulk-booking discounts are another attraction to Japanese travelers who buy package tours. Major tour wholesalers usually make block bookings of airline seats, hotel rooms, ground transportation, and visitor attractions at special wholesale prices. They can share some of the discount with their clients when they work out package tours to popular destinations. It is ordinarily more expensive for overseas travelers to buy a ticket directly from the airline and to arrange hotel accommodations and ground transportation on their own than to buy a package tour with a similar travel itinerary. This is particularly true with second-brand (economy) tours offered during nonpeak seasons and on nonpeak days. The package typically includes economy airfare, hotel accommodations (two persons in one room), a short city tour, and transfers. In some instances, economy package tours are sold for much less than the prices quoted in the tour catalog.

It is technically possible for Japanese travelers to make direct booking with airlines of their choice. However, airlines do not sell discount tickets directly to individual passengers. All airlines prefer to sign annual sales contracts with major tour wholesalers and help protect the latter's business in exchange for guaranteed business from them. Evidently, all international airlines serving Japan hesitate to compete directly against tour wholesalers and discount ticket vendors for fear of creating ill feelings among them. These airlines must have a large volume of the bulk-booking business from the large tour wholesalers in order to maintain a high load factor on all flights.

Recently "air only" discount travel agencies started selling airline tickets at a substantial discount to individual travelers. These travel companies either buy tickets directly from airlines that have empty seats on certain days or buy them from tour wholesalers that have unsold seats on certain flights. H.I.S. is one company that has successfully entered into the new market of discount air tickets. JTB also established a new subsidiary, Travel Plaza International, which handles discount air tickets only. Discount tickets are difficult to obtain during peak seasons and are not available for bookings made far in advance of planned trips.

Types of Tour Products

There are literally thousands of different package tours designed to meet the specific needs of various travel segments. The majority of package tours are "series tours" *(shiriizu tsuaa)* that are planned, organized and marketed by tour wholesalers to the traveling public. Other tours are called "order-made tours" *(tehai ryokoo),* which have itineraries and tour activities requested by a sponsoring company or association. Another type of travel is FIT (Foreign Independent Travel), which has become extremely popular among repeaters in recent years.

Twice a year Japanese tour wholesalers plan, organize, and market these series tour packages. Creation of the tour packages begins about one year prior to the release of final products. For the April–September season, the first stage of market research and tour planning begins during late spring of the preceding year. Concurrently, existing popular tour packages are scrutinized again, and the feasibility of adding new packages is considered. During the following three to four months the planning will be completed and tour components such as airline seats, hotel accommodations, ground transportation, restaurants, and sightseeing tours will be booked. Procurement of these components is generally done by the purchasing department staff at their home office in Japan, with input from their overseas branch offices. Decisions on prices are deferred until the last possible minute so that they can reevaluate market demands on various package tours. Printing of brochures begins during the early fall, and the brochures are ready for distribution in late January or early February. Preparation for the October–March season follows after a six-month interval, and the same process is repeated. Then, tour wholesalers prepare sales kits and hold orientation sessions for retail office staff and subagents' staff and begin vigorous sales of new package tours.

Series tours are literally a series of package tours to hundreds of popular tourist destinations around the world. All major tour wholesalers offer many series tours to Guam, Saipan, Hawaii, the U.S. Mainland, Canada, Mexico, the Caribbean islands, New Zealand, Australia, Europe, Hong Kong, Taiwan, Korea, China, Thailand, and Indonesia. A few major tour wholesalers even offer series tours to the Middle East, Africa, India, Central America, and the former Soviet Union. Typically, the series tours are classified by types of tour activities, lengths of stay, and places to be visited. Pricing of these tours is determined by the class of airline service, types of hotel accommodations, kinds of tour activities, and meal plans. However, the most important factor in tour pricing is the date of departure. In Japan, airfares are not only based on seasons, but also on the specific day of departure. For example, airfares for a GIT (Group Inclusive Tour) to Hawaii have more than eight different categories based on the specific date of departure from Japan.

Based on these different airfares, tour wholesalers create series tours with different prices. For example, JTB has seven different series tours to Hawaii, and Jalpak also has seven different series to Hawaii with different tour prices that are all based on the dates of departure. Honeymoon series are much higher in price, if departures are on or the day after the "good luck" days of *Taian* and *Tomobiki*. Even though they have to pay a high premium for such tours, new Japanese couples usually want to get married on either one of these days and depart for their honeymoon on that day or on the following day. Japanese couples are still very superstitious and hold onto the old custom of holding commemorative events on these days.

Typical series tours are from four to eight days in length in order to accommodate the holiday patterns of average Japanese vacationers and honeymooners. A popular Waikiki deluxe vacation tour is either six, seven, or eight days and includes round trip air transportation, a flower-lei greeting, limousine service to and from Waikiki, an orientation session, a welcome lunch, one city tour, deluxe hotel accommodations either at the Royal Hawaiian Hotel, Halekulani, Hilton Hawaiian Village, or Sheraton Moana-Surfrider, and fine dining at John Dominis or Nicholas Nickolas. The tour members can choose in advance a hotel room in a certain hotel situated on the ocean with a panoramic ocean view. If they wish, they can take additional excursion trips to the neighbor islands of Kauai, Maui, Hawaii, Molokai, and Lanai. They can also take optional tours such as golfing, scuba diving, snorkeling, sailing, deep-sea fishing, jet skiing, horseback riding, and other outdoor activities. On other days, they may also visit Pearl Harbor, the Bishop Museum, Foster Botanical Gardens, the Waikiki Aquarium, Sealife Park, the Honolulu Zoo, the Polynesian Cultural Center, and Waimea Falls Park.

For young budget-minded Japanese travelers, tour wholesalers offer very inexpensive tour series that include only air transportation, transfers to and from the airport, and economy-class hotel or condominium accommodations. The tour members are free to choose all activities on their own, and they can save money by using public transportation, eating at fast-food or family restaurants, and by shopping at discount shops. In recent years, these tours have become very popular among young Japanese who can speak some English. They join these "no-frills" tours as individuals only a few days in advance as long as airline seats are available on the departure date.

The most popular series tour is for honeymooners. Many tour wholesalers concentrate on the honeymoon market because honeymoon packages are very profitable. Japanese honeymooners join honeymoon package tours and travel in groups with many other honeymooners. They do not seem to mind the lack of privacy as much as Westerners because they are accustomed to traveling in groups from early childhood. There are many honeymoon package tours to such popular destinations as Hawaii, Guam, Hong Kong, Singapore, the U.S. Mainland, Canada, Australia, New Zealand, and Europe. The tour prices are much higher compared to other types of package tours, as these tours usually include deluxe hotel accommodations, sightseeing excursions in a private limousine, deluxe meals, and bilingual tour escort services. For example, the tour prices of a seven-day Hawaiian honeymoon on economy class air transportation range from $2,500 to $3,500 per person, and tour prices of a similar Oceania honeymoon range from $4,000 to $5,000.

Wedding package tours are increasingly popular among Japanese couples who want to get married at famous tourist destinations overseas. Because these tours are a combination of the wedding ceremony and the subsequent honeymoon tour, they usually include wedding gown and tuxedo rentals, the services of a makeup artist, hairdresser, and wedding coordinator, private limousine transportation, flowers, a Christian church wedding ceremony, and an authentic marriage certificate signed by the minister. They also include videotaping and picture taking coordinated by the staff of the tour wholesaler or its subsidiary companies.

New popular series are "Family Vacation," "Vacation for Couples," and "Deluxe Leisurely Vacation," which are designed for the respective market segments. In order to promote these series tours, many tour wholesalers now offer discounts for spouses and children during certain nonpeak periods.

Order-made tours are affinity group tours such as incentive tours, company recreation tours, study tours, school excursions, and special event tours. These tours are arranged by tour wholesalers or General Travel Agencies at the request of sponsoring companies or schools. In addition to regular sightseeing tours and shopping, these tours typically include special activities such as lectures, dinner parties, golf tournaments, field trips, or student exchange parties, depending on the requirements stipulated by the organizers. The order-made tours are organized usually at least six months in advance to ensure that all additional tour components are obtained. The tour wholesaler must help the organizer make a detailed schedule of activities for each day and make all of the necessary arrangements without fail. For almost all order-made tours, the tour wholesaler sends at least one tour escort from Japan who has been working with the organizer on the planning and execution of the tours.

FIT is a new trend as Japanese travelers become more independent. A large number of younger Japanese have traveled internationally, can speak better English, and are not as shy as older Japanese generally are. They enjoy making travel arrangements on their own and going places by using public transportation or by renting cars. In fact, many of these FIT travelers no longer need to depend on tour escorts and the local representatives of tour wholesalers for assistance. Recently, the growth of this market has been stimulated further by discount air tickets sales companies. At the same time, travel guidebooks and magazines with rather detailed information on major visitor destinations have been successful in promoting the FIT market in Japan.

Chapter 11

Initiating and Maintaining Business Contacts

Initiating business contacts with Japanese tour wholesalers and travel agents is very difficult and time consuming, to say the least. Generally speaking, most Japanese businessmen are not friendly to strangers. They prefer to do business with friends and other business associates whom they have known personally for many years. They may appear to be friendly and agreeable, but, in many instances, they become evasive and non-committal when they are forced to make quick decisions. They rely heavily on personal introduction by a reliable person or introducer *(shookaisha)*. They hesitate to enter into any new business relationship without such an introduction. They will take much more time getting to know personally each individual with whom they intend to do business. They will also require considerably more written information and data prior to engaging in any serious business discussions. Once the business relationship is initiated, they usually prefer to maintain close interpersonal contact on a long-term basis with every business associate. It is, therefore, very important to understand specific business practices that are uniquely Japanese.

Interpersonal Network Building

Building interpersonal networks of friends and business associates (this is called *kone* in Japanese) is the number one priority in starting any business relationship with the Japanese. These networks are usually made up of close friends, family members, friends of the family, bankers, business executives, directors of trade associations, government officials, and business consultants. Naturally these individuals must know both parties to be introduced, and they must be respected and trusted by each side. Their introductions are extremely important for breaking the ice and initiating a business relationship, since a casual introduction by a mutual acquaintance would have no effect at all in Japan. There are several ways to cultivate the important networks of personal relationships:

(1) Attend international tourism conferences. This is a good way to meet Japanese travel executives. These conferences are usually organized by international travel organizations, visitor bureaus, hotel associations, restaurant associations, or chambers of commerce. Some of these conferences are jointly sponsored by JATA, PATA, and other Japanese travel organizations. For example, JATA holds an international congress with a trade show every other year in November. Meetings are conducted mainly in English, and eminent travel industry experts make presentations. Seminars and panel discussions cover the highlights of the Japanese travel industry's future trends, current problems, and possible solutions. The Japanese participants who come to this congress are more open and more willing to meet and socialize with future business associates from foreign countries. They usually have a good command of English and are also looking for new business opportunities themselves. An international conference such as this one could provide excellent opportunities to initiate business with Japanese travel companies. When it becomes necessary to obtain personal introductions, one of the senior members of the conference organizers' team could play the role of introducer and lend credibility.

(2) Use of government representative offices. Most tourism-oriented countries and local governments have tourism promotion offices in Japan. For example, the United States has the United States Travel Service in Tokyo, and the Hawaii Visitors Bureau also has its own branch office there. The officials of these government offices can assist in providing proper introductions to prospective Japanese client companies, as the Japanese usually respect official introductions from governmental offices.

(3) Contacting local tour operators. Major Japanese tour wholesalers have subsidiary companies and branch offices that act as local tour operators for incoming Japanese tour groups. These offices often make introductions and are even asked to negotiate contracts on behalf of their head offices in Japan with tourist product suppliers such as hotels, restaurants, ground transportation companies, souvenir shops, visitor attractions, and other optional tour service companies. In most cases, however, final decisions are still made by the headquarters in Japan. Suppliers should approach the local branch manager or the official representative of Japanese tour wholesalers as an initial step to establishing a business relationship. This person can give proper introductions to the people in charge at the head office and provide guidance on how to approach them. This is the most effective way because the branch manager can also explain to his superiors and colleagues in Japan a new business proposal in Japanese.

Western businesspeople are often tempted to go directly to the top executives at the headquarters in Japan. This approach can be a big mistake because Japanese executives rely heavily on the judgment of local managers whenever they consider establishing any new business arrangement in a foreign country. In other words, the suppliers of tour products must win the trust and friendship of the local manager before contacting their superior at the headquarters. Naturally, local managers will not make any introductions unless they are convinced that the company will benefit from establishing new business relationships. They will be very cautious about recommending new companies because they would have to take full responsibility if something goes wrong.

(4) Cultivate friendships through civic and social clubs. Japanese businessmen join several civic and social clubs in order to make friends who will help them in their business dealings later. Popular clubs for travel executives are the Rotary Club, Lions Club, Young Presidents Organization, and Chamber of Commerce, as well as sports and hobby clubs involving golf, tennis, skiing, baseball, fishing, calligraphy, ceramics, and mahjongg. They also use "old boy" networks among the alumni of the same university. Family ties *(enko kankei)* are

often used to obtain good introductions. Nepotism is not looked down upon in Japan. On the contrary, good family ties are valuable social assets used frequently to gain instant credibility. The reason for this is that the Japanese still tend to believe that close relatives either by blood or through marriage would never betray each other.

Effective Forms of Introduction

There are several forms of introduction, such as a telephone call, a business card with a brief note, a letter of introduction, and face-to-face or personal introduction. A telephone call is obviously the most casual way, and it is used only when the parties involved are good friends. A business card with a brief note is an abbreviated letter of introduction. An introducer would write on his business card a note that might say, "This is to introduce Mr. John Smith, vice president of International Travel Service. Please give him due courtesy," and then put his seal *(han)* on it. This form of introduction is not very effective unless the introducer follows up with a telephone call. A letter of introduction is more effective because it shows that the introducer took the time to write a letter. However, it could be just a social courtesy with little impact unless the writer makes a follow-up telephone call. Although it happens only in rare instances, the introducer may contradict what was written in the letter in a telephone call later. The letter is *tatemae* (what ought to be ordinarily said), while the phone call is *honne* (what the introducer really thinks). In other words, the introducer may not refuse a request for introduction to save face, but he may call the friend to whom the letter is addressed and say something like, "I just met Mr. Smith during the JATA conference last month. Please listen to his presentation for my sake, but I cannot take any responsibility for him."

The most common and only effective method of introduction is face-to-face. Typically, the introducer arranges the initial introduction meeting at a nice restaurant at the request of the party to be introduced and invites the other party. Breakfast meetings are almost never arranged in Japan. Most businessmen commute for long distances by train from their homes in the suburbs, and business hours for offices are from 9:00 or 9:30 A.M. to 5:30 or 6:00 P.M. A business lunch is more acceptable in Japan, but it is not as effective as a dinner meeting, since a luncheon meeting does not provide enough time for socializing and exchanging information on personal backgrounds. Japanese businessmen are not comfortable starting any new business until they have gotten to know the other business associate personally.

Dinner meetings must be planned and executed carefully with proper protocol. The first dinner meeting is used only for greetings *(aisatsu)*, not for discussion of specific business matters. During the dinner, everyone engages in small talk and asks personal questions about each other. The first question is usually about the nature and length of the personal relationship between the introducer and the person to be introduced. Other questions would deal with the prospective business associates' hometown, the university from which they graduated, years of service with their respective companies, mutual friends and acquaintances, golf handicaps, hobbies, and foreign travel and sojourns. At this dinner meeting a small gift is usually given to the guest as a token of friendship. It might be a ballpoint pen with the company logo, a tie tack and cuff link set, or a bottle of imported whiskey or wine. The personal behavior of the host (who requested the introduction) will be closely watched by the invited guest during the dinner. If the guest does not like the host's attitude, personality or behavior, no further meeting will be suggested. But if this initial meeting is successful, the introducer will ask them to meet again on another occasion with or without him. The second meeting usually is a dinner hosted by the other party for more socializing.

Mailing Letters Directly

Many Western businesspeople think that they can somehow begin new business relationships by sending a letter of self-introduction with a copy of the company brochure to Japanese companies and following up with a telephone call. However, they will be very disappointed because Japanese companies do not respond to this method of solicitation for several reasons: (1) direct mailing lacks the personal touch that is an important prerequisite for starting a business relationship; (2) Japanese companies require much more information about the company and its people before they respond to any letter of solicitation; (3) most likely, letters written in English will need to be translated into Japanese before non-English speaking senior managers can read them; and (4) because decisions are not made quickly in Japan, a response could be delayed for weeks or even months.

Cold Calls

Making a "cold call" to prospective clients is a common practice among aggressive salespeople in Western countries. In Japan, the cold call is not only impolite, it is also ineffective in initiating business relationships. Almost all Japanese companies politely refuse to grant an interview to the aggressive salesperson who barges in to see top management without an appointment. *Monzenbarai* (send away at the entrance) is the usual treatment given to strangers who suddenly appear on the doorstep. In some cases, junior supervisors may be assigned to see the "intruder," and their function is to listen to the presentation for a few minutes and say something like, "I will convey your message to my superior. Please leave your business card. We will call you if we decide to do business with you." It should be obvious that the salesperson will never be called, because the junior supervisor is saying "no" in a roundabout way.

Only under rare circumstances will Japanese salesmen use a method called *ohyakudo wo fumu* (making one hundred visits) when they want to win the sympathy of the companies they have been pursuing. But they use this method as a last resort when they cannot obtain proper introductions from anyone. However, this method is obviously not feasible for foreign businesspeople making a short trip to Japan to establish a new business relationship.

Maintaining Personal Contacts

In any business relationship, maintaining personal contacts with business associates is very important. In Japan, this is the only way to ensure the continuation of any successful business relationship.

As Japanese businessmen prefer to do business with certain individuals whom they know very well, it is quite possible that a written agreement would be "conveniently" ignored when those individuals are transferred or leave the company. The most effective ways to maintain personal contacts are frequent entertainment and socializing and regular courtesy visits. In fact, Japanese companies spend a lot more money and executive time on entertainment than American or European companies. There are several forms of entertainment and socializing that are more suitable and effective with Japanese business associates.

Business Lunch or Dinner

Having business lunches or dinners does not stop at the initial introduction or even after the subsequent consummation of a contract. It is absolutely necessary to exert even more effort to nurture the interpersonal relationship over many months and years through occasional business lunches or dinners because Japanese businessmen prefer to discuss business matters in informal situations. A regular invitation to lunch or dinner is the best way to show appreciation for continuing business.

There are some important cultural factors and commonly used protocols that need to be recognized when hosting Japanese businessmen. Choosing whom to invite is the first consideration. Top executives must be matched with top executives, and middle managers with middle managers. For example, if the senior vice president is the host, he or she should invite the senior vice president of the other company. If mixing of different ranks is necessary, it is essential to match ranks carefully when seating the guests. In some situations, the host may have to sponsor a separate party for each rank, one for top executives and another for middle managers. It is acceptable for businessmen to bring wives to social dinners, but some Japanese businessmen may feel constrained and uncomfortable discussing business matters when spouses are present. Even though more and more Japanese women join their husbands for social dinners held for visiting Westerners, most of them still feel uneasy and alienated because they are not used to socializing with foreigners. In general, only those directly involved in the business should be invited to a business lunch or dinner.

A female executive may find socializing with Japanese businessmen uncomfortable or she may feel out of place if she must go to dinner and a hostess bar with them. She may also feel uncomfortable because Japanese businessmen prefer to discuss business matters between small talk, drinking, eating, and while flirting with young hostesses. In this situation, the female executive should make an extra effort to create a strong impression that she is a businessperson first and foremost. She should dress conservatively and act professionally in all of her encounters with Japanese men. It would be a good idea to have an older male manager accompany her as "special assistant" and ask him to take on the socializing usually reserved for men only.

Selecting a good restaurant is very important. Japanese businessmen almost never volunteer where they want to go for dinner. They would probably say that any restaurant is fine, but they will actually size up the host and the company by the kind of restaurant chosen. A coffee-shop type restaurant is naturally not good enough for Japanese executives with expensive tastes. Older businessmen prefer Japanese restaurants, although some of them may like Western-style restaurants. Sometimes it is a good idea to ask the guest's secretary what restaurants and types of food they like. Another good idea would be to ask them what type of restaurant they have been to lately. It is also possible to suggest a few good restaurants and their specialties and then ask guests to choose one of them.

The seating arrangement is another important factor to consider. In Japan, the highest-ranking guest is seated at the *kamiza,* which is usually a seat by a window with a nice view of the ocean or garden, away from the entrance or kitchen door. This guest may hesitate to take the honored seat right away but should be pushed into taking it. (See Chapter 6 for a more detailed explanation on proper seating arrangements.)

When menus are presented to Japanese guests, they may not immediately open them and make their choices. They may wait and observe how the host reacts to the menu items and to the specials offered by the waiter. They almost always defer to what the host recommends. Many Japanese just order a complete meal, as they do not want to bother with choosing each item individually. They are more likely to say something like, "Oh, just order the same thing for me" or "I will leave it up to you," and they rarely order the most expensive dishes out of politeness. Since it is an important Japanese social custom to hold back *(enryo)*, it is the host's responsibility to insist tactfully that the guests have something they will really enjoy. Some diet-conscious Americans often commit the cardinal sin of hurriedly ordering a large dinner salad and a cup of decaffeinated coffee, or of refusing dessert while urging the Japanese guests to have it.

In Japan, *omakase ryoori* (leave-it-to-the-chef meal) is considered the best treat. This method of ordering a meal is used by Japanese top executives when they invite really important guests to restaurants they frequently use. Their intention is to convey two distinct messages to the guests: (1) "I am an important regular customer, and the chef knows exactly what to serve my important guests"; (2) "You are my important business associates and I am offering you the best meal at this fine restaurant in Japan." In fact, the menus of some exclusive Japanese restaurants are handwritten and have no prices listed for the menu items. *Omakase ryoori* can easily be three hundred to five hundred dollars per person.

Many Japanese businessmen are heavy drinkers and chain smokers. They often start with a bottle of beer to whet the appetite, then switch to scotch and water, *shoochuu,* or *sake.* Some of them even order a bottle of expensive French wine to accompany the main dish. They may light cigarettes quite frequently during dinner, although some may refrain from smoking in the presence of nonsmokers. The constant smoking may present a problem among dinner guests who cannot tolerate secondhand smoke.

In Western countries, especially in the United States, "backslapping informality" is quite common at a dinner party. In Japan, however, the total disregard of formality and certain rituals is detrimental to starting a new relationship with status-conscious Japanese businessmen. There is an old saying, *"Shitashii nakanimo reigi are"* (Politeness is important even among the closest of friends), which means status differences must be observed in all social encounters. The dinner party always begins with a formal toast by the host. It is impolite for any of the guests to touch their drinks or eat until the host makes a brief statement appropriate for the occasion, which may be a welcome party, contract-signing party, reunion, or *sayonara* party. Juniors in rank and age should refrain from making humorous comments or telling jokes when seniors are present.

Another important ritual is that no one should pour their own drinks when drinking with others. People sitting across or on either side of the same table should always be aware when to pour more drinks for others. This must be done especially when sharing the same bottle of beer or *sake*. A common way of performing this ritual is to go around with a big bottle of beer or *sake* and to pour it into the glass or cup of other individuals with whom new relationships are to be established or old acquaintances renewed. In all instances, this ritual is initiated by a lower-ranked person, and it is accepted by the person of superior status. Honored guests will have their beer glasses filled all the time by others who wish to pay their respects. Another ritual often observed is the exchange of small *sake* cups. For example, Person A drinks from a cup of *sake*, rinses the cup in the water-filled bowl on the table, hands the same cup to Person B, and pours *sake* into this cup. Person B drinks from it and then returns the cup to Person A. This is repeated a few times. This is an age-old ritual of bonding between friends. In most instances, the waiters and waitresses are asked to assist in performing this important drinking ritual by pouring drinks. Japanese businessmen rarely relax and enjoy active conversation until they are somewhat intoxicated. They drink a lot with some appetizers before eating their main dishes.

Today many Japanese dinner parties include *karaoke* singing. Because foreign guests are also expected to display their singing talent, they should know a few English songs that are popular in Japan. It goes without saying that everyone is considered a "good" singer. All guests at the party should give loud applause for the singing.

There are two important cultural differences between Japanese and Western ways of paying the bill at the end of a dinner party. The Japanese host often has a subordinate discreetly pay the bill, while the Western host usually pays it in full view of the guests. In Japan, money is still considered "dirty," and money matters are handled by a lower-ranked person in the group. Many top executives of major Japanese corporations do not pay each time they dine at restaurants they patronize regularly. They may simply walk out, thanking the restaurant manager and the chef for a fine meal. Since their faces are like credit cards, the restaurant can bill their company at a later date. Sometimes, Japanese guests may walk out of the dining room before the host finishes paying the bill. This behavior is not considered impolite in the Japanese cultural context because the guests should not be interested in how much the host has to pay for the dinner.

In Japan, it is also customary to give a small gift to everyone invited to a dinner. This could be a box of cookies, a cake, seasoned fish or meat, dried noodles, or something else from that particular restaurant. This gift is usually meant for the guests' family members who were not invited to the dinner.

Nijikai (Second Outing)

There is a unique Japanese way of continuing the evening socializing begun at dinner. It is called *nijikai,* or "second outing," which could be puzzling (even annoying) to uninformed Westerners. Japanese businessmen usually invite their associates after dinner to their favorite bars or private clubs for more drinking, talking, and *karaoke* singing. In other words, a typical Japanese social does not end with a two-hour dinner, but is more likely to be two hours for dinner and another three hours for more drinking. In some instances, they may go for *sanjikai* (third outing) if they feel like doing so. As mentioned earlier, Japanese businessmen cannot seem to relax and talk freely until they have consumed a certain amount of alcohol. Under the guise of being drunk, they often express *honne* or say things that they think would be too impolite to say while sober. Refusing to go to a second outing is not a good idea even for nondrinkers because so-called heart-to-heart talks often occur during this outing. They might nonchalantly drop important hints on pending business matters while drinking, singing, and merrymaking. Japanese businessmen believe that at *nijikai* or *sanjikai* people usually show their true colors, and they size each other up by observing the behavior of others at this outing. They say they can often ignore etiquette *(burei koo)* when they are drinking, and they feel free to speak their minds. For example, a Japanese senior executive who did not speak very much during the formal meeting may start speaking a lot more after having a few drinks. He may even venture to express true feelings at this time. Or a junior manager may hurriedly state a personal opinion or what he thinks his superiors are alluding to when they are away from the table. Among these Japanese businessmen "I had too much to drink" can be used as an excuse for any misstatement or unbecoming behavior.

Golf Games

In Japan, playing golf regularly with business associates is the most effective way to maintain important personal contacts. All major companies own memberships in two or more famous country clubs. Executives and managers play golf games with their clients two or three times a month. These games are sometimes called *tsukiai gorufu* (obligatory golf games) because business executives must make certain that their clients are thoroughly entertained. In *tsukiai gorufu,* the hosting party should not beat the guests. They often rig the game by giving an ample handicap or by intentionally missing crucial shots. The caddies that accompany important guests are instructed to extend extra courtesy and special assistance. Some caddies are said to carry a few extra golf balls of the guests' brand and discreetly replace a "lost" ball for the benefit of the invited guest golfers.

Like dining and *karaoke* singing, golf games require four or five hours to play, during which business associates can socialize and get to know each other personally. The Japanese seem to believe that both the verbal and nonverbal behaviors of golfing partners on the golf course reflect their personalities and business acumen as well. Friendships made on the golf course also seem to be very strong among the Japanese. For example, a major duty-free shop in Hawaii requires that their Japanese customer service managers play a weekend golf game with the local managers of major Japanese tour wholesalers and travel agents. This particular strategy seems to work very well for them in retaining old customers in the face of tough competition from other stores. It is an excellent idea to sponsor annual golf tournaments to create regularly scheduled opportunities for business associates to get together. For this reason, major international airlines and large hotel chains sponsor golf tournaments and invite tour wholesalers and retailers in order to retain their clients' loyalty.

Hyookei Hoomon (Courtesy Visits)

Paying courtesy visits is one of the age-old business traditions still practiced in Japanese business. Business executives make courtesy visits to important clients (and sometimes to government offices). They generally do not have any specific business to discuss, but they are expected to make regular visits in person in order to pay their respects and show appreciation for continued patronage. These visits are made on different occasions, such as the beginning of a new year or the anniversary of a contract signing. In some ways, this is just like a courtesy visit by a high-ranking diplomat intended to promote goodwill and friendship. Therefore, *kao wo dasu,* or "showing your face," is an extremely effective way of maintaining personal contacts, especially if the "faces" are those of the top executives. When making courtesy visits, the visitors always bring with them an appropriate gift for the occasion. They may even sponsor a dinner party or a golf tournament if they feel such an event is called for.

Excursion Trips

Inviting clients to go on a short trip is another effective method used by Japanese businessmen in maintaining close personal ties. In Japan, the most popular excursion is an overnight trip to a hot-spring resort. This trip usually combines a golf game, relaxation in a hot-spring bath, and a dinner party. It may also be the only way to capture the undivided attention of busy executives. Some Japanese corporations invite important clients on golf tours to Hawaii, Guam, or Korea. Some other corporations combine an overseas inspection tour with a golf outing and sightseeing. A few days of golfing and enjoyment on an excursion can certainly help develop friendships and interpersonal trust, which are crucial in maintaining ongoing business relationships.

Written Greetings and Gift Giving

Japanese social customs call for the sending of greetings *(aisatsu)* on certain occasions such as *nengajoo* (new year's greeting) and *shochuu mimai* (midsummer greeting) in addition to the newly adopted Western custom of sending Christmas cards. *Nengajoo* are given to express appreciation for past patronage and favors received the preceding year and to solicit the same for the coming year. *Shochuu mimai* are given to enquire about the health and well-being of the recipients during the hottest months of the summer.

There are two gift-giving occasions during a year. One is *oseibo* (year-end gift), given during the month of December to give thanks for past patronage and favors. The second is *ochuugen* (midsummer gift), given during the months of July and August. Department stores and other retail shops conduct special sales during these two gift-giving seasons and offer a huge variety of gift items. *Oseibo* and *ochuugen* are usually delivered to the offices of client companies, but separate gifts are also delivered to the homes of corporate executives and managers who have done special favors in the past. It is important to note that these greetings and giving of gifts are the two most important social customs still used in maintaining and renewing personal ties among businessmen, relatives, and friends.

In addition, Japanese businessmen are expected to attend the weddings and funerals of the family members of their business associates and to give appropriate monetary gifts based on the extent of their personal relationship. In a nutshell, business relationships are much more time consuming, personal, and intimate in Japan as compared to those of Western countries.

Chapter 12
Contract Negotiation and Japanese Business Culture

Whether negotiation is conducted in English or Japanese, the Japanese negotiation style is perhaps the most distinctive. It is far different from the styles of other Asians such as Chinese and Koreans, who often engage in aggressive haggling and bargaining. The historical and cultural roots of the Japanese still influence the Japanese style of business negotiation. It is more ritualized and formal. Japanese negotiators adhere to certain rituals and several specific steps of negotiation influenced by culture and social norms in interpersonal relations. They may intentionally give vague answers, as they value interpersonal harmony over frankness. They tend to rely on an unwritten verbal agreement *(kuchi-yakusoku)* rather than on the legal language of a contract in interpreting the terms and conditions. Unlike American corporations, Japanese businesses usually do not use attorneys when they negotiate a contract because they prefer to solve disputes in a more amicable manner through renegotiation or mediation. The overly aggressive and argumentative style of negotiation often used by Western negotiators would be ineffective and disruptive, to say the least. Therefore, potential business associates must examine a number of important cultural factors in order to make negotiations with the Japanese more successful and effective.

Starting a Contract Negotiation

Business negotiations always begin with the proper introduction of each person involved. The first step is to exchange business cards *(meishi)* among those participants meeting for the first time. In Japan, the business card is treated like one's face, which makes a first impression. If the card is of poor quality or soiled, it would naturally leave a bad first impression. During the exchange, a card should be handed out to each individual as if it were an expensive and fragile gift. It should be offered right side up from the recipient's view, and it should never be handled in the manner of passing out playing cards at a card game even when several people are present. A business card serves a number of important functions in the Japanese business context. It provides the person's name, job title, department, company name, address, and telephone and facsimile numbers. It also clarifies the status relationships among those who are exchanging cards. It is important to remember that the job title, company affiliation, and age usually dictate the language usage and the manner of speaking, and a lower-status person (seller) always offers his card first to a high-status person (buyer).

The second step is to find out who, on the Japanese side, will actually negotiate and make decisions. In many instances, the Japanese businessmen who appear at the negotiation table are not necessarily assigned to negotiate. The role of top executives is ceremonial.[1] If the executives are brought early into the negotiation process, they are there for *aisatsu* and participating in small talk for ten or twenty minutes just to size up the potential negotiators. All issues are actually negotiated by the middle management and senior staff members in charge of the negotiation. Unlike their Western counterparts, Japanese top executives are usually not prepared to bargain and make any commitments on their own. Consequently, Western negotiators should not expect them to be present and actively participate in negotiation sessions. It is also impossible to persuade them on the spot with logical arguments because decisions are usually made by group consensus after a series of careful deliberations. Major decisions are still made by *ringi-seido* (group decision-making process), which requires approval from all top executives and key managers whose departments or sections will be affected by the decisions to be made.

Nontask Sounding

Nontask sounding is the nonbusiness-related conversation that takes place prior to moving on to task-related discussions. Japanese negotiators spend a lot of time on small talk and social conversation, and they always attempt to assess each participant's personality, personal background, and professional knowledge and skills. They feel that they should know everyone personally so they can anticipate their reactions and plan negotiation strategies accordingly. They usually talk about sports (mostly golf and baseball), weather, the business climate, the visitor's hometown, the long flight from home, familiarity with or what they like about Japan, and so on. The reason why they spend a lot of time for nontask sounding is that they feel they need to establish good rapport and create a friendly and amicable atmosphere for negotiation. They also feel that the negotiation sessions will move more smoothly once a good personal relationship is established.

During this stage, it would be wise for Westerners to make favorable comments about the Japanese company and its top executives whom they have read about in recent trade journals, newspapers, and magazines. For example, it would be appropriate to say something like, "I read in the last issue of *Travel Journal* that your company increased honeymoon package tour sales by 30 percent. Congratulations!" And it would be extremely helpful to have pertinent background information about the company such as the names of key executives and senior managers, locations of overseas offices, capitalization, number of employees, main products or services, sales volumes, and major stockholders. At this time, it would be necessary to present company brochures and promotional materials printed in Japanese.

Exchange of Task-Related Information

The timing of switching from nontask sounding to task-related discussions is very critical. Rushing into a business discussion prematurely is not only impolite, but it also spoils the pleasant mood and destroys the rapport established during the first phase. It is always necessary to wait for the Japanese negotiators to signal when the exchange of task-related information should start. After a second cup of coffee or tea is served, they may send a signal by saying something like, "Well, we know you are busy. Should we ask you to explain your business now?" At that moment, Western negotiators should be careful not to barge in and start a one-way communication with too much enthusiasm.

American businesspeople in particular unwittingly make statements that may make the Japanese counterparts feel offended or upset. They might say, for example, "We are the only company that can offer you the best service at the lowest price. We hope that we can enter into a contract with us right away. I'll personally take care of it if you'll sign up with me today!" Although these statements are quite appropriate in the American business context, the Japanese side would see them as boorish and arrogant. A statement referring to a future business relationship on Japanese terms is more appropriate at this time. For example, Westerners could say, "We are here to find out what we can do to assist you in your tour operations in our city" and wait for the Japanese negotiators' reaction before discussing specific issues.

At all times, Westerners must recognize and accept the possible communication difficulties caused by inadequate competency in English and differences in nonverbal behaviors. Although many Japanese businessmen in the tourist industry have a fairly good command of English, they may not be truly bilingual and bicultural.[2] In some instances, they may pretend to understand and say, "Yes, I understand" just to avoid personal embarrassment. They may also say yes when they disagree with you because in Japanese it is grammatically correct to say, "Yes, I don't agree with you." This means that American negotiators should take time and explain one major point at a time and use written materials and visual aids in their presentation.

If communicating in English seems difficult, it may be best to hire a professional interpreter. When talking through an interpreter, the negotiators should be careful not to face the interpreter all the time. Instead, they should look at the Japanese negotiators and talk to them directly. If they do not do so, they could make their Japanese counterparts feel slighted and ignored. Another social error often committed is ignoring a senior manager whose English is limited and talking more to a junior member of the staff who speaks good English. In all situations, Westerners must recognize that seniority is very important in Japan. Invariably, these unintentional social infractions may cause serious problems in contract negotiations.

Nonverbal Communication

In face-to-face negotiation sessions certain Japanese nonverbal behaviors may be quite puzzling to Westerners. The most puzzling are the so-called "Japanese smile" and "Japanese yes." A famous Japanese business consultant said, "Never take a smile for yes. Never take yes for an answer. When a foreign businessman has mastered the art of reading between the smiles and yeses, he has become a seasoned executive in Japan."[3] It is also important for Westerners to remember that the Japanese smile when they want to hide embarrassment or even anger. They may also say "yes" and nod their head to every question or request. This is called *aizuchi* (nodding), and it does not necessarily mean that they agree. It is more like "uh huh" in English rather than a definite yes. In other words, the Japanese negotiator's smile may mean, "I'm sorry, I don't really understand what you are saying, but I won't admit it because I am too embarrassed." Or it may mean, "I recognize what you are saying, but your request is ridiculous. You can't be serious." It is indeed very important to accurately understand the nonverbal behavior of the Japanese at the negotiation table.

Persuasion and Concessions

The typical Western style of negotiation, especially that of Americans, is based on the premise that negotiation is a game. Negotiators see negotiating as a series of problem-solving exercises with the ultimate goal to win the game. They come to the negotiating table with the authority to negotiate and make final decisions. They lay the cards on the table and are willing to make concessions on the spot. They enjoy engaging in open debate and heated discussions over any point of disagreement.

On the other hand, Japanese negotiators do not consider negotiation a game. They do not like to engage in open debate over difficult issues, either. They seem to behave as if they are there to continue an information exchange and to confirm what has been talked about before. They do not disclose what they have in mind until they first obtain all the information needed for them to make a decision. They would never make concessions without first reaching a consensus among themselves. In many instances, they may suddenly stop negotiations and start talking in Japanese to each other if they have a disagreement among them. Another problem is that Japanese negotiators do not follow agenda items one at a time. They often skip or delay discussion of difficult items that are preconditions for further negotiation. And if they are pressured to tackle those problems, they may either sidestep or give vague answers. They will not be impressed by arguments and persuasion based on Western logic. Instead, they would demand many more facts and data on each item of discussion when pressured to make commitments.

When negotiating with the Japanese, Westerners tend to become impatient and frustrated. They cannot sit and wait when the Japanese negotiators are slow in responding and when they remain silent for a few minutes. They never take no for an answer. Because they do most of the talking and tend not to listen, they fail to understand what the Japanese are really thinking. In some instances, they may hastily propose to "split the difference" out of desperation. A very low-key and patient approach would obviously be much more effective when negotiating with the Japanese.

Perhaps the most important cultural factor to recognize in negotiating with the Japanese is status differences. The power position in a business relationship in Japan is based primarily on the size and prestige of one company over another. Large and famous companies usually expect and receive preferential treatment over smaller and less prestigious companies. Westerners must remember that their Japanese counterparts still uphold the old Japanese concept that the buyer is king, where buyers expect to receive more deference and respect than sellers. Status-oriented Japanese buyers naturally demand more concessions and services. For example, a major Japanese tour wholesaler may be more demanding and difficult to negotiate with if the foreign supplier of tour products is a small company.

There are two Japanese cultural factors, *amae* (indulgent dependency) and *nagai tsukiai* (long-term relationship), that are frequently used in the negotiation process. These are rather difficult for Western businesspeople to understand. *Amae* means that the sellers can indulge in their dependency on the buyers, even though buyers can demand whatever deal they want. In other words, the buyers are expected to take on an implicit responsibility to consider the financial needs of the sellers. The sellers can often succeed in negotiations by humbling themselves and begging persistently.[4] They need not worry that they will be taken advantage of by the buyers and lose everything. In fact, the sellers know that they will make "enough money," an amount considered appropriate by the buyers. Japanese negotiators frequently use the statement, "We are going to have a long-term relationship" as the reason for asking for further concessions. They really value long-term relationships that will continue to bring benefits to both sides, but, at the same time, this can be just an excuse to take advantage of the negotiating opponents.

Another unique Japanese negotiation tactic is "you go first," or making the contingent offer. They never disclose their own negotiation positions first without knowing their opponents' positions. In other words, they make concessions or compromises only if the opponents do so first. The Japanese abhor making unilateral concessions or giving up something for nothing. If they are forced to make concessions, they may demand even a token concession in return in order to save face.[5]

Reaching an Agreement

Trying to reach an agreement and obtain a commitment from Japanese negotiators during a negotiation can be very frustrating. In many instances, they say yes when they mean maybe or no because they almost always say what they think their opponents want to hear. They do not openly express their *honne* (true feeling) if the answer is negative because they want to maintain interpersonal harmony and avoid personal embarrassment, particularly in face-to-face negotiation sessions. There is a famous story about an aggressive New York businessman who completely misunderstood the "Japanese yeses and smiles." He boasted to his superior that he had successfully negotiated a super deal with a major Japanese company in Tokyo after a series of hard bargaining sessions and arm twisting. When he returned to New York, he was shocked to find a facsimile message waiting for him on his desk. The message read, "We regretfully inform you that we must cancel the whole deal" with no explanations at all. He was dumb-founded because he thought everything had gone so well in Tokyo. The New Yorker reported that the Japanese negotiators had said yes to all of his demands and even smiled a lot. Appar-ently his aggressive American negotiation tactics had backfired on him. How could he have avoided this big mistake? One obvi-ous solution could have been not to push the Japanese too hard and force them to make a decision before they were ready. He could have paid close attention to what the Japanese side was really trying to communicate, instead of dominating the negotia-tions by engaging in one-way communication.

Japanese businesses still use *ringi-seido,* which requires many weeks of *nemawashi* (informal consultation) among the individu-als and departments that will be affected by the pending decision. This means that repetitious negotiation sessions are necessary in order to facilitate consensus. Some negotiation team members are routinely replaced in the same manner that players are rotated during a basketball game. If they cannot reach consensus easily with their counterparts, new negotiation teams may be assigned to repeat the negotiations on the same agenda that were already discussed at length with the previous negotiation team. In certain crisis situations, the president of a company may suddenly exercise the ultimate power and reject the agreement single-handedly. This action would negate the agreement that has been reached by group consensus. If this happens, the Japanese negoti-ators would be forced to say something like, "We are sorry. Our president said no." And they would not offer any legitimate rea-sons as to why the agreement was rejected. On the other hand, if the negotiations are going as planned, the president may show up during the last phase of negotiation to give his blessing.

Still another problem in reaching an agreement with the Japanese is that government bureaucrats and bankers may inter-fere with this process. Japanese bureaucrats have always had a strong influence on how international business is conducted, especially when Japan's national interests are at stake. They are very protective and will interfere with any international business deals that might seriously threaten the interests of any Japanese companies. Japanese bureaucrats have been known to have blocked implementation of free-trade pacts. For example, importation of fruits and meat products as *omiyage* is subjected to extremely time-consuming inspections and approval procedures for no specific reason.

Banks in Japan also have a very strong influence on the decisions of the companies that receive financing from them. In many Japanese corporations, executives and senior managers in charge of finance and accounting are former bankers who have had dealings with the members of these corporations before retirement. (They are called *amakudari* or "heaven descent.") The roles of these bureaucrats and bankers cannot be ignored when negotiating with Japanese companies. They are the "hidden" negotiation opponents who can exert considerable influence, although they may not be physically present at the negotiation table.

Japanese-Style Contracts and Their Enforcement

The traditional Japanese attitude toward the written contract has been that it is merely a tangible acknowledgment of a relationship between two parties. Most Japanese businessmen assume that rights and duties written in the contract are provisional or tentative rather than absolute. They often recognize the doctrine of *jijoo henkoo* (changed circumstance), which means that the specific terms of a contract are open to renegotiation whenever unexpected changes may occur in the future.[6] Business contracts in Japan, therefore, are much shorter and less detailed compared to Western-style contracts.

Almost all Japanese-style contracts include a clause that says, "Any future disputes shall be settled by mutual consultation. Both parties promise to do their utmost to resolve such disputes." Another commonly used clause is, "All other items not covered in this contract shall be deliberated and decided in a spirit of honesty and mutual trust." This is exactly the reason why Japanese negotiators do not argue about what one specific word, phrase, or sentence should mean in the contract to be signed. In most cases, contracts are deliberately written loosely and contain only major provisions. For the Japanese, what has been talked about and verbally agreed upon during the negotiation sessions is more important than what has been written on paper. All participants on both sides are expected to remember *kuchiyakusoku* (unwritten verbal agreements) and the atmosphere under which they have come to an agreement. In other words, *kuchiyakusoku* is just as important as a written contract, and it could become the basis of interpretation and implementation for that particular contract in the future.

Apparently, Japanese businessmen probably would not like a typical American-style contract with very detailed terms and conditions. They know that American lawyers participate in business negotiations from the beginning and go to great lengths to protect their clients against all contingencies and every possible legal ramification. The Japanese detest such a practice, as the lawyers seem to work on the assumption that the contract will not be honored or that at least part of it will be violated anyway. A prominent Japanese executive once remarked, "An American business contract is like a prenuptial agreement. It actually spells out conditions for a divorce before the two lovers are married. Why should they get married in the first place, if they know that the marriage is not going to work out?" It is very clear that undue emphasis on minor details of a contract will cause suspicion and uneasiness on the Japanese business associates. In Japan, it is considered unwise to include legal advisors in the early stage of contract negotiation and let them take over the discussion.

Obviously, there is no simple answer as to which type of contract should be used. It depends on the size, complexity, and importance of the agreement, as well as the parties involved. Managers of large Japanese firms with many years of international business experience understand the necessity of having a detailed contract when doing business with foreign companies. They may even ask for an American-style contract with detailed terms and conditions drawn up by lawyers. They will then have their own legal counsel review it carefully because they are aware of the frequency of litigations and the cost of defending them in court.

One Japanese businessmen's tendency that seems peculiar to Westerners is that they often sign a contract without reading it carefully. They may simply ask, "Does this contract include all the things we talked about and agreed upon?" And if the answer is affirmative, they will sign it without checking it again carefully. They usually trust that the other side will not trick them into signing a one-sided contract once a strong personal tie is established through many days of socializing and negotiation.

On the other hand, the same Japanese businessmen will not hesitate to ask for modifications or the cancellation of the original contract, even if it has already been signed and sealed. As mentioned earlier, they feel *jijoo henkoo* (changed circumstances) almost automatically entitle them to ask for changes. For example, a Japanese tour wholesaler has a contract with a major resort hotel. The contract calls for 500 rooms at $100 a day during the annual high peak seasons; an advance deposit of $100,000 is payable at the time the contract is signed, with a 50 percent non-refundable deposit made three months in advance, and full payment 30 days prior to actual occupancy. Due to "unexpected economic circumstances," the tour wholesaler finds it impossible to fulfill the terms of the contract. In this case, the Japanese managers who negotiated this contract will go back to the hotel management and ask for a reduction in the number of reserved rooms at very short notice. They will try to convince the hotel management not to charge any late cancellation charges. They might insist on the change in the contract by saying, "We should help each other when one of us is in trouble. We will have a long-term relationship." They expect the hotel managers who were involved in the initial negotiations to accept this request and to take a big loss of revenue without any monetary compensation. The managers are expected to recognize that the tour wholesaler had the intention of honoring the contract and has made every effort possible. They are also expected to remind themselves that the managers of the tour wholesaler, as buyers, have superior status to that of the hotel managers, who are the sellers.

Having a formal contract-signing ceremony is another unique Japanese business custom. The Japanese like to have a signing ceremony similar to that held for a diplomatic treaty. If the contract to be signed involves a major capital investment, the ceremony is an elaborate and expensive one. It would be attended by top executives of both companies, the main banks' representatives, the local media, trade association leaders, and local government officials. The ceremony is usually held in a hotel banquet room and is followed by a lavish reception. Commemorative gifts are exchanged and souvenirs are given to those who attend the signing ceremony. It is important to choose appropriate gifts for the occasion because they will become important mementos for each participant. Even for a small contract a dinner party to celebrate the signing is in order. Apparently, such a signing ceremony adds goodwill and a positive emotional touch to the impersonal written contract.

Handling Contract Disputes

In Western countries, especially in the United States, business disputes are almost always handled by attorneys. Businesses and even individuals do not hesitate to file suits and countersuits to settle contractual disputes. In contrast, Japanese businesses prefer to settle their disputes without going to court. They rarely sue each other, as they view business relationships as very personal in nature and they always try to avoid public disclosure of any disputes. The Japanese businessmen involved not only find litigation distasteful, but also feel ashamed to have created such a situation in the first place. They would rather compromise and settle out of court in order to avoid public embarrassment and the bad publicity of a long legal battle. The most preferred methods of handling contract disputes are *hanashiai* (consultation), *chuukai* (mediation), and *chuusai* (arbitration).

Consultation

Informal consultations over dinner and drinks are the first step in resolving any business dispute in Japan. Instead of hiring legal counsel immediately, the parties that negotiated the original contract will call an informal meeting to discuss the matter. This meeting can be easily arranged because Japanese businesses usually keep up the relationship in a personal manner rather than a strictly businesslike one.

After signing a contract, the beneficiary side (the host of the signing ceremony) will send a formal letter to the other side expressing pleasure and confidence that the new relationship will be prosperous and long lasting. The host company will also send pictures of all of those who participated in the negotiation sessions and other social events, including dinner parties and golf games. This personal touch is an important reminder of the camaraderie and friendships developed during the weeks and months of negotiation and socializing.

Another important Japanese practice is *hyookei hoomon* (courtesy visits). Top executives of both sides make frequent visits to each other in order to keep the relationship warm and personal. Good communication through these visits can prevent small problems from developing into serious ones. If a problem should arise due to drastic changes in circumstances, the visiting executives will know about it, and action will be taken to resolve it immediately. The rationale for this approach is that those who actually negotiated the contract remember *kuchiyakusoku* (unwritten verbal agreements) and can work out a mutually acceptable solution to any future contractual disputes. If any of the original members has been transferred to another department, they should be included in future meetings as observer or advisor. If this is not possible, they should at least be invited to social events. The Japanese executives will be disappointed if they cannot renegotiate the contract with their old friends.

It is also important to remember that the initial discussion of disputes be conducted at *jimu reberu* (staff member's level) without any executives present. This is an important means of saving face for the executives who negotiated the original contract. Only after they have come up with a few mutually acceptable solutions will the staff members in charge consult top executives for advice and endorsement of the best alternative. It would be unacceptable to find the Japanese executives who appear to be in charge and talk to them directly because all important decisions are by group consensus in Japan.

Mediation

If consultation and renegotiation between the parties do not work, mediation will be the next step in resolving a contractual dispute. In Japan, assistance from a *shookaisha* (introducer) or *chuukaisha* (mediator) will be sought. The introducer may act as mediator if called upon to do so. A mediator usually is a *yuuryokusha* (man of influence), a powerful politician, an executive director of a trade association or an international business consultant, but not a lawyer. The mediator must have good *ningen kankei* (human relationship) with the members of both parties and must also be known as a neutral and fair-minded person with personal credibility and power. The mediator will listen to claims or complaints from each side and analyze them objectively in an effort to mediate the differences. Instead of dealing with legal interpretations of the terms and conditions of the contract, a typical Japanese mediator will try to persuade both sides to accept an amicable solution based on emotional ties and mutually beneficial business opportunities in the future.

Arbitration

Arbitration is the third step in resolving a contractual problem. The Japanese Commercial Arbitration Association (JCAA) conducts hearings on disputes, but arbitration proceedings are very difficult and extremely time consuming and the arbitration by JCAA may not produce the desired outcome. Because the most-favored Japanese approach to resolution is through cooperation and compromise, it is reported that only 1 percent of all cases brought to the JCAA result in binding arbitration.

In recent years, the Japanese also have begun to use litigation to solve legal disputes, but this method should be used as a last resort. As explained earlier, the Japanese prefer informal means of settling disputes to antagonistic confrontations in court. Although comprehensive legal codes and rules for commercial transactions do exist in Japan, legal interpretations are based on a blend of imported Western legal concepts and Japanese social traditions.

Indeed, the Japanese legal system as it appears on paper is quite similar to the Western system. It is dangerous to assume, however, that these imported legal codes and practices will be applied in settling international disputes. Japanese lawyers hesitate to file lawsuits because they feel that every effort must be made to settle them before going to court. Even if they file lawsuits for their clients, they will continue to do their best to settle out of court. Many Japanese lawyers even believe that individual interests should be voluntarily sacrificed for the sake of social harmony. The Japanese government also promotes the use of less disruptive means when it comes to settling international disputes.

This means that litigation cases filed in Japan may literally take years before any settlement is reached.

It is possible to hire American lawyers in Tokyo who specialize in the legal aspects of international business, but they cannot function as efficiently and effectively in Japan as they could in their own country. The best advice to Western businesspeople is to avoid filing lawsuits and to seek solutions to contractual disputes with Japanese business associates through consultation and mediation.

Appendix I

Top Twenty Japanese Travel Agencies

Japan Travel Bureau, Inc. (JTB)
1–6–4, Marunouchi, Chiyoda-ku, Tokyo 100
Phone: (03) 3284–7028

Kinki Nippon Tourist Co., Ltd. (KNT)
19–2, Kanda, Matsunaga-cho, Chiyoda-ku, Tokyo 101
Phone: (03) 3255–7111

Nippon Travel Agency Co., Ltd. (NTA)
Shimbashi Ekimae Building
2–20–15, Shimbashi, Minato-ku, Tokyo 105
Phone: (03) 3572–8717

Tokyu Tourist Corporation
Shibuya Chikatetsu Building
1–16–14, Shibuya, Shibuya-ku, Tokyo 150
Phone: (03) 3407–0121

CO-OP Travel Service
Sanko Building
1–1, Kagurazaka, Shinjuku-ku, Tokyo 162
Phone: (03) 2325–0510

Meitetsu World Travel, Inc.
Taiyo Building
8–8–5, Ginza, Chuo-ku, Tokyo 104
Phone: (03) 3572–6371

Kankyu Express International Co., Ltd.
3–3–9, Shimbashi, Minato-ku, Tokyo 105
Phone: (03) 3508–0127

Nishitetsu Travel Co., Ltd.
3–16–26, Yakuin, Chuo-ku, Fukuoka 810
Phone: (092) 524–3521

JALPAK Co., Ltd.
Boeki Center Building Annex
2–4–1, Hamamatsucho, Minato-ku, Tokyo 105
Phone: (03) 3435–6521

Tobu Travel Co., Ltd.
Nichido Yaesu Building
3–4–12, Nihonbashi, Chuo-ku, Tokyo 103
(03) 3624–1231

Yomiuri Travel Service
Yomiuri Shimbun Daiichi Bekkan
2–2–15, Ginza, Chuo-ku, Tokyo 104
Phone: (03) 3563–6431

Yusen Air & Sea Service Co., Ltd.
Sanshin Building
1–4–1, Yurakucho, Chiyoda-ku, Tokyo 100
Phone: (03) 3592–1265

Nankai Travel International Co., Inc.
1–10–4, Nanbanaka, Naniwa-ku, Osaka 556
Phone: (06) 641–6000

Nisshin Travel Service Co., Ltd.
Bussan Building, Annex 3rd Floor
1–1–15, Nishi Shimbashi, Minato-ku, Tokyo 105
Phone: (03) 3595–1230

Union Overseas Corporation
Osaki New City Ichigo-kan
1–6–1, Osaki, Shinagawa-ku, Tokyo 141
Phone: (03) 3779–7711

JETOUR, Inc.
Tokyo Club Building
3–2–6, Kasumigaseki, Chiyoda-ku, Tokyo 100
Phone: (03) 3502–0131

Kokusai Kogyo Travel Service
7–109, Ginza, Chuo-ku, Tokyo 104
Phone: (03) 3575–0881

Keio Travel Agency Co., Ltd.
Shinjuku Sumitomo Building
2–6–1, Nishi Shinjuku, Shinjuku-ku, Tokyo 163
Phone: (03) 3344–1801

Keihan Travel Service Co., Ltd.
Osaka Green Building
3–1, Kitahama, Higashi-ku, Osaka 541
Phone: (06) 202–3528

Zenkan Tour Service Co., Ltd.
Kydo Building
1–5–4, Yaesu, Chuo-ku, Tokyo 103
Phone: (03) 3274–4511

Appendix II

Major Japanese Travel Industry Associations

Japan Association of Travel Agents (JATA)
Zennittsu Kasumigaseki Building
3–3–3, Kasumigaseki, Chiyoda-ku, Tokyo 100
Phone: (03) 3592–1271

Japan Guide Association
#917, Shin Kokusai Building
3–4–1, Marunouchi, Chiyoda-ku, Tokyo 100
Phone: (03) 3213–2706

Japan Travel Bureau Foundation
1–6–4, Marunouchi, Chiyoda-ku, Tokyo 100
Phone: (03) 3584–7115

Japan Travel Writers' Organization
5–16–5–208, Roppongi, Minato-ku, Tokyo 106
Phone: (03) 3432–7383

The Leisure Development Center Foundation
9th Floor, Toranomon Mitsui Building
3–8–1, Kasumigaseki, Chiyoda-ku, Tokyo 100
Phone: (03) 3504–3325

Overseas Hotel Executive Association
#1211, Win Aoyama
2–2–15, Minami-Aoyama, Minato-ku, Tokyo 100
Phone: (03) 4302–3012

Overseas Tour Operators Association of Japan
2nd Floor, Izumi Building
2–20–30, Takanawa, Minato-ku, Tokyo 108
Phone: (03) 3445–7891

Tour Conducting Service Association in Japan
4th Floor, Daimon Nagahashi Building
2–2–6, Shibadaimon, Minato-ku, Tokyo 105
Phone: (03) 3432–6032

Travel Agency Fair Trade Council
5th Floor, KRF Building
1–5–5, Kyobashi, Chuo-ku, Tokyo 104
Phone: (03) 3272–7633

Japan National Tourist Organization (JNTO)
10th Floor, Toyo Kotsu Kaikan Building
2–10–1, Yurakucho, Chiyoda-ku, Tokyo 100
Phone: (03) 3216–1901

Japan Hotel Association
Shin-Otemachi Building
2–2–1, Otemachi, Chiyoda-ku, Tokyo 101
Phone: (03) 3279–2706

Japan City Hotel Association
Kogyo Building, 43
Kanda-Higashi, Matsushitacho, Chiyoda-ku, Tokyo 100
Phone: (03) 3258–1090

Japan Tourist Hotel Association
1–8–3, Marunouchi, Chiyoda-ku, Tokyo 100
Phone: (03) 3251–5330

Japan Minsyuku Association
Sukegawa Building
4–10–15, Takadanobaba, Shinjuku-ku, Tokyo 169
Phone: (03) 3364–1855

Japan Restaurant Association
Ginza 8-chome Juban Building
8–10–8, Ginza, Chuo-ku, Tokyo 104
Phone: (03) 3571–2438

Japan Education Center for Hotel Industry
3–10–12, Higashi-Nakano, Nakano-ku, Tokyo 164
Phone: (03) 3360–8231

Notes

Chapter 1: Reasons for Overseas Travel

1. *The 1992 Kankoo Hakusho* (1992 White Paper on Travel) (Tokyo: Prime Minister's Office of Japan and the Japanese Ministry of Finance, 1992), p. 25.

2. 1992 *Kankoo Hakusho,* p. 10.

3. 1992 *Kankoo Hakusho,* p. 22.

4. The *Mainichi* Newspapers "On Overseas Air Travelers," Marketing Intelligence Corporation (Japanese Overseas Travelers' Index), quoted in *JTB REPORT '94: All about Japanese Overseas Travelers* (Tokyo: Japan Travel Bureau, 1994), pp. 24–25.

5. *1992 Kankoo Hakusho,* p. 99.

6. *1992 Kankoo Hakusho,* p. 33.

7. *JTB Report '92: All about Japanese Overseas Travelers* (Tokyo: Japan Travel Bureau, 1992), p. 22.

8. *1992 Atlas of the World* (rev. 6th ed.) (Washington, D.C.: National Geographic, 1992), pp. 126–127.

9. Quoted in *JTB REPORT '93: All about Japanese Overseas Travelers* (Tokyo: Japan Travel Bureau, 1993), p. 8.

10. *JTB REPORT '92,* p. 35.

Chapter 2: Visitor Attractions and Sports Activities

1. N. Leiper, "Japanese Travel Market and Its Potential for Australian Tourist Destinations," research study commissioned by Qantas Airways, Ltd., Sydney, Australia, 1985.

2. *1992 Kankoo Hakusho,* pp. 172, 319.

3. *Rejaa Hakusho '93* (1993 White Paper on Leisure: Post Bubble Leisure) (Tokyo: Leisure Development Center, 1993), pp. 10–11.

Chapter 3: Visitor Profile and Market Segmentation

1. *The 1994 Kankoo Hakusho* (Tokyo: Prime Minister's Office of Japan and the Japanese Ministry of Finance, 1994), p. 52.

2. *JTB Report '94,* p. 13.

3. Kazuo Nishiyama, *Japanese Tourists Abroad* (Honolulu: International Management Consultant, 1973), p. 14.

4. *JTB Report '92,* p. 46.

5. *1992 Kankoo Hakusho,* p. 52.

6. *JTB Report '94,* p. 13.

7. Ken Schooland, *Shogun's Ghost: The Dark Side of Japanese Education* (New York: Bergin & Garvey, 1990), p. 21.

8. *1992 Kankoo Hakusho,* p. 151.

Chapter 4: Promotion Media and Other Promotion Strategies

1. *1992 Kankoo Hakusho,* p. 23.

2. K. Nishiyama, *Strategies of Marketing to Japanese Visitors* (Needham Heights, Mass.: Ginn, 1989), p. 13.

3. *JTB Report '94,* p. 49.

4. *1991 Visitor Satisfaction Report: Part 5, Publication on Readership Behavior* (Honolulu: Hawaii Visitors Bureau, 1991), p. 61.

5. *JTB Report '94,* pp. 42–43.

6. Ibid., p. 42.

Chapter 8: Air Transportation and Local Sightseeing Tours

1. *Weekly Travel Journal,* special 1995 summer issue (June 19, 1995): 10–12.

2. R. L. James, "Asia-Pacific Travel Trends and Implication," paper presented at The 9th Japan Congress of International Travel, Takanawa Prince Hotel, Tokyo, Japan, December 1, 1993.

Chapter 9: Nonverbal Communication in Customer Contacts

1. J. Condon and K. Kurata, *In Search of What's Japanese about Japan* (Tokyo: Shufunotomo Co., Ltd., 1987), pp. 62–63.

Chapter 10: Japanese Travel Agencies and Tour Products

1. Japan Travel Bureau Foundation, *Trends in Travel Market— Annual Edition 1992: Actual Condition of Travel and Forecast* (1992), p. 64.

2. Tokyu Tourist Corporation and Hankyu Express International formed a new joint venture company called VITA in 1993. They market and service all of their overseas package tours under the VITA label.

3. Japan Travel Bureau Foundation, *Trends in Travel Market*, p. 65.

4. 1993 *Nippon Keizai Shimbun Kaisha Soran* (Directory of nonpublic corporations) and 1994 *Toyo Keizai Kaisha Shikiho* (company directory).

5. *JTB Report '94*, pp. 35–40.

6. Ibid., p.38.

7. *The Golden Age of Travel* (Tokyo: Japan Travel Bureau, 1992).

8. *Our Profile* (Tokyo: Jalpak Co., Ltd., 1992).

Chapter 12: Contract Negotiation and Japanese Business Culture

1. J. L. Graham and Y. Sano, *Smart Bargaining: Doing Business with the Japanese* (Cambridge: Ballinger, 1984), p. 70.

2. K. Nishiyama, "Japanese Negotiators: Are They Deceptive or Misunderstood?" *Human Communication Studies*, vol. XXII (June 1994): 164–178.

3. M. Imai, *Never Take Yes for an Answer: An Inside Look at Japanese Business for Foreign Businessmen* (Tokyo: The Simul Press, 1975), pp. 76–77.

4. T. S. Lebra, *Japanese Patterns of Behavior* (Honolulu: University of Hawai'i Press, 1986), pp. 80–81.

5. M. Blaker, *Japanese Negotiating Style* (New York: Columbia, 1979), pp. 179–184.

6. R. M. March, *The Japanese Negotiator: Subtlety and Strategy beyond Western Logic* (New York: Kondansha, 1988), pp. 111–112.

Glossary of Japanese Terms

aisatsu	greeting session or greeting
aiseki	seating with a stranger
aizuchi	nodding
amae	indulgent dependency
amakudari	"heaven descent" (retired banker/bureaucrat)
anata	you (common form)
anata-sama	you (very polite)
anshinkan	sense of comfort
an'ta	you (not polite)
apetaizaa	appetizer
Bensai Gyoomu Hoshookin	Compensation Security Bond
biiru	beer
chaahan	fried rice
chippu	tip
chirashi	advertisement insert
choorei	pep-talk session in the morning
chuukaisha	mediator
chuusai	arbitration
chuusaisha	arbitrator
dantai waribiki	group discount
docchi	which (very informal)
dochira	which (formal)
dokushin kizoku	"bachelor royalty" (nickname of rich single woman)
dore	which (informal)
Eigyoo Hoshookin	Business Guarantee Bond
endaka	high yen value
enkai	drinking party
enko kankei	family ties
enryo	holding back
furonto	front desk
futon	Japanese-style bedding
futsuu tsuuwa	station-to-station call
gyooza	pot sticker (fried dumplings)
hakuraihin	goods brought by ship (imported goods)
han	seal, stamp

hanashiai	mutual consultation
hansei kai	review meeting (of study tour)
hatsumono	the very first crop
hikidemono	return gift for wedding guests
honne	what one really thinks
hyookei hoomon	courtesy visit
ian ryokoo	company recreation trip
Ippan Ryokoo	
Gyoosha	General Travel Agency
irasshaimase	welcome (greeting to you)
jijoo henkoo	changed circumstance
jimu reberu	staff member's level
juken juku	cram school (preparatory school)
jukensei	student preparing for entrance exam
juusu	juice
kaisuiyoku	ocean-water bathing
kakuteru	cocktail
kamisama	god
kamiza	the best seat for honored guests
kankoo	sightseeing
kanpai	cheers, bottoms up
kao ga kiku	having strong personal influence
kao wo dasu	show one's face
karaoke	accompanying music for social singing
katakana	Japanese phonetic writing
kekkon soodanjo	matchmaking service for single persons
kekkon yuwai	monetary wedding present
kenshuu ryokoo	study tour
kimi	you (informal)
kinen shashin	souvenir photo
Kokunai Ryokoo	
Gyoosha	Domestic Travel Agency
kokusai kankoo	
hoteru	international tourist hotel
kokusai sensu	sense of internationalism
kone	interpersonal network
kuchiyakusoku	unwritten verbal agreement
kyooiku mama	education mother
maedo arigatoo	
gozaimasu	thank you for your continued patronage
makunouchi bento	Japanese-style box lunch
meibutsu	famous products
meishi	business card

menyuu	menu
miai kekkon	arranged marriage
mikaku	taste
mikoshi	portable shrine of Shinto god
miso	bean paste
miyagebanashi	souvenir stores from travel experience
mizuwari	scotch and water
monzenbarai	send a visitor away at the entrance
mooningu kooru	wake-up call
nagai tsukiai	long-term relationship
nakoodo	marriage go-between
nemawashi	informal consultation
nengajoo	new year's greeting card
nijikai	second outing
ningen kankei	human relationship
Nokyoo	Japan Farmers Cooperatives
nyuugaku yuwai	celebration for entrance into school
ochuugen	midsummer gift
ohanami	cherry blossom viewing
oheya ni tsukeru	charge to one's room
ohyakudo wo	
fumu	making one hundred visits
okaeshi	return gift
okaimono kaado	shopping card
okyaku-sama	Mr./Mrs./Miss Customer
omae	you (very informal)
omakase ryoori	leave-it-up-to-the-chef meal
omiyage	souvenirs
omiyage ten	souvenir shop
onomimono	alcoholic drinks and other beverages
orei	token of appreciation
oseibo	year-end gift
otaku-sama	you (very polite)
otomodachi	friend
otsumami	snacks, appetizer
pachinko	pinball machine
raisu	rice
ramen	noodle dish
ren'ai kekkon	love marriage
ringi-seido	group decision-making process
ryokoo gyoomu	
toriatsukai	
shunin	certified travel consultant

saabisuhin	small gift, giveaway item
sanbaizu	soy sauce with vinegar and lemon juice
sanjikai	third outing
sashimi	sliced raw fish
sei'i	sincere attitude
senbetsu	monetary gift (given to travelers)
senmonten	specialty store
sen'poo barai	collect call
shayoozoku	businesspeople with a large company expense
account	
shimei tsuuwa	person-to-person call
shinjinrui	new breed of young Japanese
shiriizu tsuaa	series tour
shochuu mimai	midsummer greeting
shoochuu	white liquor
shookaisha	introducer
shootai ryokoo	incentive tour
shuugaku ryokoo	annual school excursion
shuushoku yuwai	celebration for getting a first job
sochira-sama	you (extremely polite)
sotsugyoo yuwai	celebration for graduation
sumimasen	I'm sorry
sumo	Japanese wrestling
tabi	travel
taian	lucky day (peace and safety)
tajuu hoosoo	bilingual format
takkyuubin	home delivery service
tanabata	star festival (July 7th)
tatemae	what ought to be said in public
tehai ryokoo	order-made tour
teisai	outward appearance
teishisei	low posture
temee	you (very impolite)
teppan yaki	hot-plate cooking
tomobiki	lucky day (friendship and harmony)
tsukiai gorufu	obligatory golf (to entertain clients)
tsumi horoboshi	
ryokoo	repentance tour
uisukii	whiskey
waribiki	discount
wasabi	Japanese green mustard
yuuryokusha	man of influence

Index

 Production Notes

Composition and paging were done in
FrameMaker software on an AGFA AccuSet
Postscript Imagesetter by the design
and production staff of University of
Hawai'i Press.

The text typeface is Baskerville and the
display typeface is Antique Olive.

Offset presswork and binding were done by
The Maple-Vail Book Manufacturing Group.
Text paper is Glatfelter Smooth Antique,
basis 50.